SOCIAL ISSUES AND LIBRARY PROBLEMS
Case Studies in the Social Sciences

SOCIAL ISSUES AND LIBRARY PROBLEMS

Case Studies in the Social Sciences

BY KENNETH F. KISTER

Simmons College, School of Library Science

R. R. BOWKER COMPANY, *New York & London* • 1968

PREFACE

The purpose of this collection of case studies is to train librarians for professional work with the literature of the social sciences. Because case studies raise questions rather than give answers, the book has no thesis or message except that social science literature has its own logic, its own justifications, and is, in general, a source of problems for professional librarians. Underlying the book, however, is the basic assumption that librarians studying social science literature will be better prepared to confront the literature and the problems it engenders if the case study method of instruction is used as a complement to traditional teaching methods. This assumption rests on my conviction (not original, and shared by many others) that professional library work of any kind, on any level—if it is genuinely professional—necessarily involves administrative activities such as decision-making, problem-solving, planning, and supervision, and that the case method provides a highly effective means to prepare librarians for these activities.

There is nothing esoteric or difficult about the case method. It is essentially a heuristic (or problem-solving) approach to learning, and while its format and application vary somewhat depending on who is using it, the definition found in *Webster's Third New International Dictionary*—an instructional method which "presents for observation and analysis actual recorded or current instances of the problem under study and often calls upon the student to render practical help"— clearly describes the case method as perceived by teachers in such diverse fields as law, business, public health, international relations, psychological warfare, public relations, and library science. Likewise, its basic aim or objective, which Arthur Stone Dewing in his valuable essay on using case studies in *The Case Method at the Harvard Business School* (edited by Malcolm McNair, McGraw-Hill, 1954) has expressed as "training to enable the individual to meet in action the problems arising out of new situations of an ever-changing environment," is un-equivocal and uncomplicated.

When E.M. Forster used the phrase "only connect" to preface *Howards End,* he was implying that some of us live in a void, failing to relate our lives to the business of living. In educational terms, the case method attempts to connect the study of librarianship with the business of being a librarian. It presents the library student with specific problem situations or case studies involving both theoretical and prac-tical questions pertaining to library work which require extensive anal-ysis and solutions based on relevant documentation or supporting evi-dence. Because case problems have no established or official "answers," the student is expected to consider opposing viewpoints germane to the issues he identifies and to explore the advantages and disadvantages of possible solutions. Evidence to support his arguments and decisions may be drawn from any number of formal or informal sources, including published literature, original investigation such as interviews with spe-cialists and telephone surveys, past or present work experience, and information gained from study in other courses, in or out of the library curriculum. Finally, the student is judged on the quality of his analysis, the depth of his research, and his ability to arrive at viable, defensible solutions based on that analysis and research.

As mentioned previously, the thirty case studies in this book have been designed for librarians studying the literature of the social sci-ences. Those using the book as a text will quickly discover that I have placed considerable emphasis on situations which confront the stu-dent with bibliographic problems. This emphasis is deliberate, reflect-ing my belief that the first requirement for professional librarians who work with social science literature is an understanding of the formal bibliographic system which provides access to the literature and its con-tents. Understanding the system—its composition, limitations, strengths, idiosyncrasies, potential—not only enables the librarian to achieve biblio-graphic mastery over the literature, within the possibilities of the system, but it also becomes the basis for professional judgments regarding the se-lection, acquisition, organization, and retrieval of the literature. For example, in case thirty, in order for Hathaway to do his job—make decisions, solve problems, supervise, and so on—he must be fully cognizant of the bibliographic scheme of things as it pertains to the literature of the social sciences and, in regard to Pike's proposal, specifically the literature of education. The same can be said of Itasca in case two, or Miss Tunneman in case five, or Flint in case twenty-one.

In some instances, cases which appear at first glance to be simple, straightforward fact-finding questions have more complex aspects to them. Case twenty illustrates this point. Ostensibly, it concerns locating factual information about applicants denied admission to college because of past histories of mental illness; but after the student has checked the obvious statistical compilations and fact-finding tools and found that data are not readily available on the subject, as he doubtless suspected from the outset, a bibliographic search utilizing both formal and informal channels becomes necessary—unless, of course, the student decides that further investigation is not warranted and can successfully defend that position.

In a few instances, cases deal exclusively with the social sciences rather than the literature itself. These case studies, of which case twenty-nine is an example, are included so that the student will have some frame of reference when he considers why the bibliographic system controlling social science literature is as it is. Certainly there is little doubt that a causal relationship exists between the unique historical nature and development of the social sciences as fields of study and the evolution of the bibliographic network librarians encounter when working with the literature of the social sciences. Just the simple fact that social science research tends to be non-cumulative, in contrast to the physical sciences, which ruthlessly discard their past, has huge implications for anyone concerned with social science bibliography. Therefore, if the librarian is to understand the bibliographic system, particularly its current state, well enough to be its master, he will require some fundamental knowledge of the characteristics of the social sciences.

The case studies in this book are not limited, of course, to bibliographic aspects of the literature. Some cases pose problems concerning selection and acquisition of materials. For example, case six asks the student to develop a genealogy collection for a small public library; case fourteen concerns the feasibility of establishing an oral history collection in a research library; and case twenty-five involves expanding the holdings of current foreign language publications in English translation in an academic library. Other case situations engage the student in the reference aspects of the literature. Still others raise the ever-popular, ever-present issue of overt or implied censorship.

I should also point out that the cases are in no special order as they appear in the book. Because a well-constructed case frequently involves a number of related issues—case thirteen, for instance, concerns both the question of censorship and evaluation of reference materials on Negro history—arrangement by type of case was not considered. And, while the thirty case studies do cover literature in the areas of business and economics, education, history, political science and international relations, psychology, and sociology, arrangement by subject would have been folly, given the interdisciplinary nature of the social sciences. Thus, to borrow a favorite word of social scientists, the arrangement is random.

Using these case studies as a teaching device allows the instructor a great deal of freedom in actual classroom application and making assignments, but it also requires a certain flexibility on his part. Whether the instructor assigns twelve or fifteen cases a semester for oral discussion, asking students to prepare their analyses in note or aide-memoire form; another three or four cases for written presentation (see the five sample student analyses appended to case thirty); requires ten short written papers, using these as the basis for discussion; or uses the cases in an impromptu fashion by assigning them to be read and analyzed in class without prior research, is not terribly important, as long as he is comfortable with the arrangement. What is important, however, is that the instructor using case studies be willing to accept points of view which do not coincide with his own, and that students be encouraged to express their own ideas without thought of pleasing the instructor. Classroom discussions stimulated by case studies are most effective when the instructor suppresses his natural desire to dominate and acts as a guide, keeping the discussion relevant and the lines of communication open. If the instructor has absolute wisdom and many great truths to give his students, the case study method should not be used.

Perhaps the most important feature of the case method—however it is used and in whatever courses—is that students are responsible for thinking for themselves, rather than having predigested opinions and attitudes handed to them. Certainly, if the historian Arthur Bestor Jr. was right when he surmised that "Genuine education consists in the communication not of conclusions but the power to reach conclusions," then the philosophy of the case method is sound.

Much more, of course, could be said about the case study method and the case studies which make up this collection. Regarding the latter, I am content to rely upon the good judgment and common sense of those who will be using the book to clarify for themselves any points which I have left unexplained. Indeed, to say more might inhibit experimentation and innovation with these cases by other instructors. However, regarding the case method and its general application to library education, I refer the reader to both Kenneth R. Shaffer's *Library Personnel Administration and Supervision* (Shoe String Press, 1963) and Thomas J. Galvin's *Problems in Reference Service* (R. R. Bowker, 1965). Each of these books contains a valuable introduction to the case method. Professor Shaffer began experimenting with case studies for teaching library administration at Simmons as early as 1951, and it is accurate to say that without his advice and encouragement this collection would not have been attempted. Professor Galvin's successful application of the case method to teaching basic reference also influenced my thinking, and to him I am grateful for many helpful suggestions.

Some of the problem situations in this book were drawn from personal experience or problems reported in the professional literature; however, a sizable number originated from professional colleagues in the field who were willing to share their experiences with me. I thank them sincerely. I should add also that in each instance the real situation has been disguised to protect the innocent and the guilty. All names of librarians and most place-names were taken from *Cram's New-Indexed Street Map of the Boston Area.*

I am also indebted to Paul Brawley, Miss Virginia Clark, Miss Edith Hathaway, C.M. Keen, Jr., and Mrs. Joan Shepardson—all former students—for kindly permitting me to use their analyses of case thirty as examples; to Miss Karen Dern and Miss Gayle Kerner of the Simmons College, School of Library Science staff for their secretarial help in connection with the manuscript; and to Henry O. Marcy IV, a friend and fellow teacher, for reading and criticizing the manuscript.

My obligation to John N. Berry III of Bowker's Book Editorial Department is enormous. He supplied expert guidance from an editorial standpoint, ideas for case studies, and—most important to me—encouragement. As is traditional, my wife, Suzon, appears last, but not least. Suffice it to say she helped.

Kenneth F. Kister

CONTENTS

• FOR SUZON •

INTRODUCTION

Controlling Social Science Literature*

In the novel *The Late George Apley,* John Marquand's eponymous hero sadly observed near the end of his life that "When everything is totalled up we have evolved a fine variety of flushing toilets but not a very good world"—a judgment difficult to refute, and, if anything, more valid today than when the old gentleman recorded it. Certainly, since Apley's day, man's mastery over the physical world (including the atom) has become just that much more incontestable while his ability to solve or ameliorate social problems has become increasingly suspect. That this growing imbalance between technical and human achievement might ultimately be disastrous for mankind—consider Gerald W. Johnson's "icy possibility" that "the force that devastated Hiroshima is really insignificant by comparison with the force that devastated the district of Watts in Los Angeles" or Buckminster Fuller's conclusion that "man on earth is now clearly faced with the choice of Utopia or Oblivion"—is gaining credence among thoughtful people everywhere, and, more specifically, forms the implicit rationale of much of the research currently being conducted by political scientists, economists, sociologists, historians, educators, psychologists, and other social scientists concerned with human behavior and institutions. The Big Question of whether or not man can or will survive is, of course, unanswerable. The smaller but related question, that of whether or not social science has the wherewithal to explain and redirect the ter-

---

* Portions adapted from the author's editorial "The Literature of the Social and Behavioral Sciences," CHOICE, III (April, 1966), 99-102.

rifying energy released in the Watts riots, or help create a utopia which will save mankind from itself, or even contribute effectively to the evolution of (in Apley's words) a better world, is not less difficult to assess and every bit as speculative. At the end of the last century, Lester Ward, that social scientist deluxe, posed the same question when he wondered, "Is it true that man shall ultimately obtain dominion of the whole world except himself?" Much as he wanted to, Ward never found a completely satisfactory answer to the question. And neither have contemporary social scientists.

There is indeed good reason to doubt that social scientists will ever obtain dominion over man. Historically, the social "sciences" —as a group of recognizable academic disciplines investigating various social phenomena—date their origins from the eighteenth century, when the first conscious, albeit often casual, attempts were made to subject so-cietal man and his activities to the same kind of disciplined, empirical scrutiny which the natural world had been undergoing successfully since the Renaissance. However, while the physical and biological sciences have continued to flourish unabated with one spectacular ac-complishment following another, the social sciences have produced thus far few genuine scientific data from which accurate and convincing generalizations can be made about man's fundamental motives and ac-tions. In the main, the results of social research have been fragmentary, superficial, contradictory, and unauthoritative—and, as a consequence, largely dismissed as inconclusive or ignored as insignificant. Bertrand Russell, never one to mince words, put the case somewhat more bluntly some years ago when he characterized the social sciences as little more than "enterprises of methodical guessing," and more recently *The Economist*, the distinguished London weekly, offered much the same opinion: "The most precise of the 'social sciences' today is probably economics, and any economist would be the first to admit that this is not saying much. Compared to economics, the other social sciences in action often look like surgery must have looked before William Harvey explained the circulation of the blood."

Doubtless it is true, as *The Economist* alludes, that the relatively late emergence of the social sciences as identifiable fields of study ac-counts—at least in part—for their ineffectual results. Not only have the several disciplines lacked sufficient time to develop mature theory and test and retest their major working hypotheses but, in addition, many of the most persistent obstacles to conducting effective social research—ambiguous and jargonized terminology, constant subject fragmentation, conflicting and confused goals, internecine quarrels concerning status and prerogatives, poorly developed data collection procedures and facilities, awkward and unreliable methodology, inadequate bibliographic access to the literature, niggardly financial support, feelings of inferiority and defensiveness when compared with the more prestigious natural sciences—derive directly or indirectly from their youthful condition. It seems a reasonable assumption that as time passes and the fields mature many of these vitiating problems will disappear (or be mitigated) in the process, thus improving the quality and authority of social science. Nevertheless, the nagging suspicion remains that man—naturally cussed, ambivalent man—is simply not a proper or hospitable subject for scientific analysis, and that the basic impediment to an efficacious science of man is more a matter of methodology than history.

For want of visible alternatives, and because of their putative commitment to scientism, social scientists have emulated the logical and quantitative methods used by the natural scientist. Quite obviously, the physical and biological sciences (especially the "hard" sciences— chemistry, physics, mathematics) are concerned with phenomena which respond to logical analysis and quantitative measurement, where one, two or three variables can be isolated and investigated separately, and the quantified bits eventually put together to form a complete picture. The social (or "soft") sciences, on the other hand, have as their subject man—multivariable, ornery, contrary man—who is too complex, too nonstatistical in nature, to be quantified precisely, who proves to be alogical as often as logical, who protects himself at will from unwelcome or embarrassing observation and experimentation, and who, as a result, does not lend himself and his social functions readily to measurement, classification, prediction, or the formulation of "laws." As Barzun and Graff note in *The Modern Researcher*, "A chemist uses a purified sample of a substance and argues after a few tests that under the same conditions all samples will behave alike. The sociologist, in imitating the chemist, samples mankind, which is hard to purify, and he seldom reaches the same results twice." Added to this dismal business is the fact that those who study human behavior are human themselves, and, therefore, are to one degree or another influenced in their problem selection and interpretation of results by the cultural, moral, economic, and political context in which they work. Studying man scientifically is nothing short of a methodological nightmare. The problems—inherent in man himself, as subject and investigator—seem insurmountable, and dominion a happy but unattainable dream.

It might seem strange then that social scientists today are optimistic—almost brazenly so—about their role for the future. The growing conviction, expressed by Dr. Edmund Volkart of the American Sociological Association, that "the first third of this century belonged to the engineer, the second third to the molecular biologist and nuclear physicist, and the final third will belong to the social scientist" pervades current thinking. And despite the many and varied difficulties associated with subjecting man to the rule of science, there are several justifications for this buoyant mood. Most obvious is the postulate that the increasingly nervous and disordered condition of modern society has correspondingly increased the relevance of social science. Social scientists (as human beings) are presumably as distressed as anyone else by the extraordinary social dilemmas which plague contemporary man, but they do believe (as professionals) with Dr. Volkart that "It's clear that the basic problems confronting our society are social problems and they can't be solved without us." At long last, social scientists are beginning to feel needed and wanted—and even indispensable.

But a much more concrete justification for optimism on the part of social scientists is the rapid development of computer technology. With its ability to handle enormous amounts of data (the possibilities are seemingly limitless) at ultra-high speeds with near-perfect efficiency, the computer holds out the prospect that quantification, where it is feasible, can be greatly improved. No one (including social scientists) seriously believes, of course, that human nature and social institutions can be reduced to a series of statistical propositions no matter how many data are available for manipulation, but in so far as the social sciences do permit quantitative analysis (and some fields, such as economics, are more responsive than others) the use of computers will vastly simplify and encourage the gathering and processing of more and more pertinent factual information. In this connection, two eminent social scientists have recently called for—quite apart from one another—the development of systematic data collection centers. Kenneth Boulding, in *The Impact of the Social Sciences*, suggests that "a world network of social data stations, analogous to weather stations" should be established. "They would take constant measurements and readings of the social system around them by standardized and carefully sampled methods and feed this information into a central processing agency." And Harold D. Lasswell, writing in *Saturday Review*, points to the need "to organize a network of social observatories capable of obtaining the information needed to choose among the theoretical models of how social changes are to be understood." Without the advent of computers, these suggestions would be merely visionary; as things stand, however, they are quite practical and possible.

The availability of computers is also beginning to stimulate increased interdisciplinary research among the social and behavioral sciences. Traditionally, the individual fields have been rigidly compartmentalized, due in part to the belief that specialization is a prime requirement of true science, and in part to the problems involved in integrating and interpreting multidisciplinary data. As the computer makes it feasible to handle greater and greater masses of information, the potential for cooperative research efforts by specialists from different subject areas is dramatically increased, and in certain fields—urban sociology, for example, where all the social sciences come into play at one point or another—this type of cooperation is not only desirable but essential. Indeed, if the cyberneticists are correct (and there is no reason to believe that they are not), computer-like equipment will eventually diffuse and blur all conventional subject boundaries, permitting something very close to what is now being called a general systems approach to behavioral study. Norbert Wiener, to whom this concept owes so much, has admitted in *God & Golem, Inc.* that "the social sciences are a bad proving ground for the ideas of cybernetics—far worse than the biological sciences, where the runs are made under conditions that are far more uniform on their own proper scale of time," but he takes pains to qualify this judgment by adding: "This does not mean, however, that the ideas of cybernetics are not applicable to sociology and economics. It means rather that these ideas should be tested in engineering and in biology before they are applied to so formless a field." The so-called "Cybernetic Revolution" is still in its infancy. Nevertheless, it offers the promise of a major breakthrough in research in social and behavioral science.

Social scientists are encouraged, too, by the increased financial support their research has been receiving of late, especially from the Federal government. In 1967, when Senator Fred Harris's bill to establish the National Foundation for the Social Sciences was being considered, *Trans-action* commented that, "Social science has had its foot in the door in Washington for some time, but now it stands a chance of getting its head in, too." At the present time, Federal money for social research is placed at approximately $400 million per year, with every indication that this figure will increase substantially in the years to come. There are, to be sure, innate dangers in government-sponsored research in the social sciences. In an editorial regarding the creation of the National Foundation, *The New York Times* asked: "Could social scientists financed by the proposed foundation really work in freedom from fear of Congressional reaction to unpopular conclusions they might reach?" One response to this problem has been the establishment of "think tanks" or institutes which, while supported principally by government funds, are operated without government interference. Sensitive issues remain unsolved concerning the uneasy relationship between social science, which needs money and integrity to function effectively, and the Federal government, which has money and a vested interest to protect; however, social scientists are genuinely confident that safeguards can be found which will insure unbiased results.

The versatility of the computer, the stimulus of money for research, and the notion that social problems "can't be solved without us" have combined to produce a generation of confident social scientists, and currently their investigations are probing every aspect of modern life—racial attitudes, sexual customs, crime, mental illness, the effects of poverty, school dropouts, marriage and divorce, personal alienation, the causes of war—not only for explanations and descriptions of human behavior but for solutions to the problems as well. Increasingly, the social scientist is thinking of himself as an "action-intellectual"—a policy-maker—rather than a "scientist" who maintains a detached, disinterested point of view. The social scientist in the latter third of the twentieth century agrees with Ralph Ross and Ernest Van den Haag when they say that, "What we know about the causes of the business cycles, for example, may be used directly to avoid or minimize economic depression. The harm done by unplanned technology . . . is not overcome by still more unplanned technology; if it can be overcome, or minimized, it will be by use of the knowledge provided by the social sciences. We can use knowledge of the conditions of daily social life and human responses to [make] changes in it, for example, to alter our traffic routes, create psychological tests for drivers, even replan our cities." Certainly considerable doubt exists that the findings and recommendations of social scientists are being accepted or implemented by those who have the final word concerning public policy (for example, one of the major conclusions of James Coleman's nationwide study for the Office of Education, *Equality of Educational Opportunity*, was that, by and large, class size has *no* effect on learning by students, with the possible exception of language study; yet this finding, based on data involving some 650,000 students and well over 60,000 teachers from more than 3,000 schools, has had no visible impact on educational policy, at least as of this time—in fact, the only concrete response to the Coleman Report by many educators has been attacks on its reputed methodological shortcomings). Notwithstanding, there is no doubt whatsoever that social scientists today are busier, more numerous, more productive, bolder, and happier than they have ever been before.

✻   ✻   ✻   ✻   ✻   ✻

As human beings, all of us are interested, quite naturally, in what social science might reveal about ourselves and our society. Moreover, as professional librarians, we are concerned with social science for what it can tell us about the behavior, attitudes, and condition of our public, be that public the general community, the academic community, or an even more specialized community of, say, businessmen, scientists, industrial researchers, or newspapermen. But, as librarians (or documentalists or information scientists—there should be no distinction), our principal concern with social science is to control the literature and information generated by the several disciplines.

The librarian's main job today—in all subject areas, not only the social sciences—is to assist in the overwhelming, often frustrating task of making knowledge accessible through such distinct though interconnected functions as selection, acquisition, classification, storage, retrieval, and circulation of literature and information. Just as the social scientist seeks dominion over man, the librarian seeks dominion over knowledge. How successful librarians are in achieving mastery or control over knowledge varies with the type and level of literature or information being sought, the form in which it is published (if published at all), and the individual librarian's ability to utilize effectively the existing control system (which has grown up without the benefit of central planning, and, therefore, is duplicatory, inconsistent, incomplete, and frequently as unpredictable as man himself). For example, a library patron seeking a book on the life of Francis Joseph, the Austro-Hungarian monarch, or Napoleon III will probably have little difficulty getting what he wants; another patron seeking the contents of a particular letter from Francis Joseph to Napoleon III may not be so lucky. On the surface, these two requests are not all that dissimilar; however, closer investigation reveals that each of these requests requires an entirely different set of research procedures, simply because the type and level of information is different, the form of publication is different, and the control apparatus necessary to meet the first request is relatively simple and easy to use while in the latter instance it is complicated, haphazard, and idiosyncratic.

Traditionally, librarians have relied on printed bibliographic tools—indexes, abstracts, book catalogs, card catalogs, monographic bibliographies, union lists, checklists, and the like—as their chief means of access to literature and information (with a variety of fact-finding tools also available as sources of precise information). Librarians have long realized that this system of bibliographic control is imperfect, and is likely to remain imperfect. As Robert B. Downs and Frances Jenkins note in their introduction to the symposium *Bibliography: Current State and Future Trends:* "Perfect bibliographical control would imply a complete record of the existence and location of every book, every document, every article, even every written thought. The probabilities of ever reaching such a utopia are remote." Indeed, the exponential growth of published knowledge—which has reached incredible proportions in the twentieth century (one estimate suggests that 500,000 pages of print are currently being added to the world's store of knowledge *every minute*)—is constantly outstripping available bibliographic resources, and unless new sources are continuously developed or old sources expanded, the system is always closer to breakdown than perfection. It has been seriously suggested, in fact, (most notably by Derek J. de Solla Price in *Little Science and Big Science*) that modern society might eventually smother itself intellectually under a mountain of technical reports, seminar proceedings, journal articles, scholarly reprints, books, documents, field studies, reviews, newsletters, and so forth. Thus far, however, librarians and bibliographers have been able to keep one small step ahead of the paper deluge.

The elaborate but strained bibliographic system managed by librarians is least trustworthy when approached by subject—or, as Downs and Jenkins put it, subject bibliography "has always been and continues to be the weakest link in the chain of bibliographical control." Quite obviously, of course, the degree of sophistication of subject control varies considerably among the major areas of knowledge—the natural sciences, social sciences, and humanities—and among the individual fields and sub-fields which comprise them. And for good reason. Patricia Knapp expressed it best, perhaps, when she pointed out that "while there are communication needs and purposes common to all disciplines, the nature and degree of bibliographic control characteristic of any one discipline is likely to depend on its maturity, the extent to which its work is cumulative, the economic support society is willing to give it, and the social structure in which its practitioners work." If we accept these assumptions as correct, it becomes very clear why the physical, biological, and engineering sciences are so much better controlled bibliographically than the social sciences or humanities. Certainly, in the case of the social sciences, there appears to be a direct relationship between the historical and current limitations of social science—late development, dubious and conflicting results, amorphous structure and nomenclature, propensity for fragmentation and disunity, pervasive (or overlapping) concerns, non-cumulative (or non-progressive) nature, lack of massive financial support, and general lack of status—and the erratic, immature condition of social science bibliography. The fact that *Chemical Abstracts* dwarfs any comparable service in the social sciences is not due to bibliographic chance but rather to essential differences in the nature and development of chemistry and the individual social sciences as fields of study. Bibliographic resources reflect the traits of the disciplines which spawn them. Or, if not that, they exhibit inherited tendencies.

A recent study conducted by the International Social Science Institute and published as *Blueprint for Bibliography* (Clio Press, 1965) found evidence of "bibliographic chaos" in the social sciences, principally because "printed reference tools are not keeping pace with the growth of literature." This does not mean that new tools are not being produced or existing ones improved; in fact, an unprecedented number of new social science bibliographies has appeared during the last ten to fifteen years. For instance, UNESCO's annual four-volume series *International Bibliography of the Social Sciences*—which provides valuable selective coverage of current monographic and periodical literature in anthropology, economics, political science, and sociology—commenced publication in the early fifties. *Current Sociology, Economic Abstracts* (the Hague), *Historical Abstracts, International Political Science Abstracts,* and *Sociological Abstracts* also came into existence during the fifties. And more recently, such major current bibliographic sources as the American Economic Association's *Index of Economic Journals, Journal of Economic Abstracts,* Harvard University Law School Library's *Annual Legal Bibliography, America: History and Life* (a sister publication to *Historical Abstracts*), *The ABS Guide to Recent Publications in the Social and Behavioral Sciences,* and the *Index to Current Periodicals Received in the Library of the Royal Anthropological Institute* have been added to the control system. In addition, of course, countless retrospective bibliographies—both general and specialized—were published during this period, including the American Historical Association's *Guide to Historical Literature* (1961), *Encyclopedia of Business Information Sources,* Miller's *The Negro in America,* the *International Encyclopedia of the Social Sciences* (fine selective bibliographies accompany the articles), White's indispensable *Sources of Information in the Social Sciences,* and new editions of Coman's *Sources of Business Information,* the *Harvard List of Books in Psychology,* and the Burkes' *Documentation in Education* (formerly *How to Locate Educational Information and Data*).

But despite all of this bibliographic accretion of the last few years (only a fraction of which is noted above) and the existence of such older tools as *A London Bibliography of the Social Sciences* (the largest general bibliography in the area), *Social Science and Humanities Index, PAIS Bulletin, Psychological Abstracts,* the *International Bibliography of Historical Sciences, Writings on American History, Foreign Affairs Bibliography, Education Index,* and *Business Periodicals Index,* there is solid evidence to support the claim that bibliographic control of social science literature has grown steadily worse instead of better, as the ISSI study indicates. The bibliographic system has simply been outrun and overwhelmed by the exponential productivity of today's energetic, confident social scientists. Moreover, the demand for information (bibliographic and otherwise) has increased significantly, both in volume and type. (Especially spotty is control of fugitive materials—multilithed, mimeographed, or photoduplicated reports, newsletters, unpublished texts of speeches, and other forms of non-copyrighted material—and foreign publications, both of which are of growing importance to social scientists and their research.) The many new bibliographic services developed for the social sciences since the fifties have doubtless saved researchers, students, and librarians alike from being engulfed by an unmanageable flood of paper a la Price, but the effort has not been sufficient to put the bibliographic house of the social sciences in order. "Chaotic" is still the best descriptor.

If the only problem confronting social science bibliography were coping with the exponentially expanding literature and information produced by and for social scientists, the remedy would be relatively simple: develop more tools faster, until the bibliographic capability to control the output equaled the output itself. Unhappily, the problem (and hence the solution) is not that simple. Bibliographic chaos in the social sciences is as much the result of the present multiplicity of sources as it is the rapid growth of the literature. Two decades ago, Margaret Egan, after arguing that "Bibliographic organization is the very life blood of a system which is essentially unitary, which resists dismemberment," warned that we must avoid "those centrifugal forces which threaten the atomization of the bibliographic process. . . . Fragmentary services are usually short-lived, but every failure makes eventual success more remote and more difficult to achieve." Notwithstanding the desirability of an integrated control system, bibliographic development in the social sciences—emulating that of the disciplines themselves—has tended naturally and consistently toward fragmentation (or atomization). The ill-fated *Social Science Abstracts* (1929-33) serves as a tangible reminder that schism, not unity, has been the story of social science bibliography. The result has been that access to literature which is pervasive in content or of multidisciplinary interest (and a considerable portion of social science literature falls into these categories) becomes more a matter of luck than of systematic control; that wasteful and uneconomical duplication occurs; that planning for improved or extended control is seldom undertaken, let alone effected; and that the bibliographic system (if we dare call it that) possesses neither a uniform internal arrangement nor a recognizable external organization. Little wonder that recent user studies reveal that social scientists would rather satisfy their informational needs through informal channels.

There are those who are working to replace or reorganize the present, unsatisfactory bibliographic system which covers the social sciences. Among these are Eric Boehm, editor and publisher of *Historical Abstracts* and *America: History and Life,* and Alfred de Grazia, who edited the initial volume of *The ABS Guide to Recent Publications in the Social and Behavioral Sciences* and founded the *American Behavioral Scientist.* Boehm, whose major recommendations are contained in

Blueprint for Bibliography (a study which he directed), calls for the creation of "one integrated, comprehensive international bibliographical system for the social sciences and humanities" which would supplant the existing "multiplicity of partial or inadequate or overlapping bibliographical efforts." As envisioned, this system would comprise various types of tools so that both selective and comprehensive control could be achieved. De Grazia, on the other hand, has gone even further than Boehm, in so far as his system, the Universal Reference System, is currently operational and available to social scientists, students, librarians. While still in its early stages of development (limited at present to bibliographies in sub-disciplines of political science), URS published volumes will eventually provide access to "significant" material in the social and behavioral sciences through intensive indexing. Designed as both a current awareness and a retrospective searching tool, URS emphasizes interdisciplinary as well as methodological aspects of the literature. Less ambitious than the proposed system outlined in *Blueprint for Bibliography* (URS does not provide comprehensive control), de Grazia's System nonetheless is built on a thorough understanding of the plight of social science bibliography. And in many respects, both Boehm and de Grazia appear to be headed in the same direction.

There are legitimate doubts, however, about just how quickly the existing bibliographic network—formless and ineffectual as it is—will yield to such new, centralizing ventures. Not only do instigation and operation of a viable bibliographic system represent a substantial financial undertaking—Boehm's plan is predicted on support forthcoming from the Federal government, similar to that accorded the NASA documentation system and MEDLARS, and de Grazia's URS appears to be self-supporting (at least his article in the February 1967 issue of the *American Behavioral Scientist* strongly implies this)—but there are vested interests represented by current services which undoubtedly will work to maintain the present system. These interests, of course, would be by no means motivated solely by financial considerations; indeed, pride in a particular service, reservations concerning the utility of new indexing procedures and classification schemes, fear of domination of one field by another, concern about possible government interference or control, and simply dedication to the status quo might all play some part in promoting resistance to a centralized bibliographic system.

Whether changes in the system governing access to social science literature and information come about slowly or rapidly, we can be certain of the fact that they will surely come. And just as the computer is on the threshold of revolutionizing social science research, so is it holding out infinite possibilites for improved and expanded literature and information control. One of Boehm's chief recommendations is "Use a computer as part of the bibliographic process, and put it to work for a large variety of tasks," and the cornerstone of the Universal Reference System is the computer, which supplies the bound bibliographies in the series (printed by offset directly from computer print-outs) as well as on-demand bibliographies to subscribers. The increasing production of Keyword-in-Context (KWIC) bibliographies, the development of Selective Dissemination of Information (SDI) systems, and the introduction of automatic indexing and abstracting are all results of the versatility of the computer. "There is a computer in your future," Jesse Shera has written, "there is no doubt about that."

The social sciences have come a long way since Lester Ward wondered if man would ultimately obtain dominion over the whole world except for himself. Attitudes have changed, techniques have changed, the men have changed, and the tools have changed. But the basic problem remains unchanged. The same can be said of librarians and their job.

1

Is There Really A Science Of Man?

"Ink? No, I'm sorry, but we don't supply ink in the library. You'll
have to go to the bookstore. Sorry."

"OK, thanks anyway. Er, maybe you have a pencil I could borrow?"

"Sure. Here. Just put it on the desk when you're finished."

Ralph Burt, reference librarian at Colwell College, watched the tri-
umphant student return to his carrel. Burt recorded a precise tick in the
reference log under "directional questions." While the pencil loan
hardly constituted a "directional" question, it fit no other category in the
log as well, so he decided to force the entry rather than consider the
intellectual proposition of to-enter-or-not-to-enter: the obligations of accurate data-keeping converged with the massive unimportance of the
whole transaction. Just as he had finished, five students—obviously
together—approached his desk. One of the students emerged from the
phalanx to act as spokesman for the group.

"Excuse us, sir. Mr. Burt?"

"Yes. What can I do for you gentlemen?"

"We're from Professor Lee's Science Club, and he said you may be
able to help us locate some information about the social sciences."

"Be glad to. Just what sort of information do you want? The social
sciences cover a lot of territory, you know."

"Well, it's like this, Mr. Burt. We're going to debate about how social
scientists—really I guess it boils down to just how scientific the social
sciences really are. This is for a Club meeting—the debate—in two
weeks. Really, I guess anything on how scientific methods can be applied to studying society and behavior—human behavior."

1

"My background's in sociology, and I'm surprised that you haven't encountered that question in your basic sociology course?"

"Well, this came up at our last Club meeting, sort of gratuitously. And since most of us are in physics and chem—"

"We have some people from bio, too, Dick." Another student came forward to help the spokesman.

"That's right. Some are in bio. Anyway, most of us don't have to take sociology. It's an elective for us. Anyone here had soc?"

Before any of the students could reply, Burt stood up. "There's certainly plenty of material available, although I think you'll find the question a bit passé now. Social scientists have resolved it—at least to their own satisfaction. I would suggest that you begin with the *International Encyclopedia of the Social Sciences*. Come on, I'll show you where it is. It'll give you something of an overview of the nature of social science methodology. Here it is. And this old set," Burt pointed to the *Encyclopedia of the Social Sciences*, "will be useful from the historical point of view. Some of you can consult *Social Science and Humanities Index* —on the periodical index shelf, over there, near the *Readers' Guide*. It's like the *Readers' Guide*—and *Applied Science and Technology Index*, which you may be familiar with—except that it indexes leading journals in the social sciences, such as *Social Research* and the *International Social Science Journal*. Let's see. Another source which could be helpful is the *ABS Guide to Recent Publications in the Social and Behavioral Sciences* and its annual supplements. By the way, the supplements are kept up-to-date by the periodical *American Behavioral Scientist*, which is in the periodical room. Look in the middle section for current books and articles. Finally, don't forget the card catalog. Look under "Social Sciences" first and cross-references will do the rest. A couple of titles I can think of offhand which you might want to get ahold of are Chase's *Proper Study of Mankind*—"

"What's his first name?"

"Stuart. And Lynd's—Robert Lynd's—*Knowledge for What?* Lynd's sort of old, but don't let that bother you. One other suggestion might be to see Dr. Foster in the sociology department. He ought to be able to give you some good ideas off the top of his head."

Several days later, Burt received a telephone call from Dr. Samuel Lee, an assistant professor in the physics department at Colwell. Burt knew Lee as a young, enthusiastic man whom he occasionally talked with in the faculty dining room.

"Richard Owen, one of the members of my Science Club, said you had been very considerate to the group the other day, showing them reference books and so on. I don't know if the boys mentioned or not that we propose to stage a debate on the question of how 'scientific' are the *social* sciences. Since my—"

"Yes, one of them did mention that, I believe."

"Since my field is physics, I'm not really conversant with *social* science. Naturally, I couldn't give the boys much guidance about what they ought to read by way of preparation. Of course, I have my *own* ideas on the subject. Now—"

"This interests me, Dr. Lee. My background is in sociology, and I'm wondering how in the world you ever got onto this question. Isn't your Club concerned with physical science mainly?"

"Almost exclusively—until now!" Lee chuckled into the phone. "Actually, it's a long story, but I'll make it brief. The other week the Club prepared a discussion about lasers—strictly from a pure science standpoint. The possibility of scattering of light by light, destruction of the classical vacuum theory, optical pumping—that sort of thing. Toward the end of the meeting, one of the boys brought up the possible practical applications of laser beams to medicine—surgery, X-ray, and so on —when greater control and power levels are developed. This took us pretty far afield from theoretical physics, but the meeting was almost over and I let the discussion roll along. Then someone got into communications applications—one laser beam has more information-carrying capacity than all radio and television channels now in existence, did you know that?—and before I knew it, we were on the effects of technology on society."

"You must have a bunch of talkers in that Club of yours."

"In all innocence—just to terminate the meeting—I said something like 'let's leave that one to the *social* scientists, boys'—"

"And *that* started the whole social science debate idea?"

"It sure did. Young Chase—Dave Chase—whose father is a cybernetician started in on methodology in the social sciences, 'laws' of human behavior, predictability—to make a long story short, everyone got excited about it, and we decided, since we are a *science* club, to investigate the *social* sciences and the validity of their so-called 'scientific' techniques."

"The idea sounds exciting, Dr. Lee. And while I think I'm safe in saying that social scientists themselves no longer argue this question—at least not as vehemently as they once did—the subject ought to get your clubmen into some very interesting areas."

"That's what I thought."

"A thought does occur to me. Why not invite a speaker, or several speakers, from the campus to talk to the Club? This would—"

"We—I—never do that. I want the boys to discover things on their own. And besides, some of these social scientists get terribly wrapped up in their own jargon—they have no sense of *lingua franca*. For instance, young Owen went to see Foster in sociology yesterday and his vocabulary snowed the boy. I'm afraid he didn't come away with anything but an appreciation of the language difficulties between him and Foster."

"Well, each discipline has to develop a specialist vocabulary. I know that all the social sciences are frequently criticized for this, but—"

"Actually, what you're saying touches on my reason for calling you, Mr. Burt. You see, although the boys were most appreciative of the books you showed them the other day, they have had *some* time trying to exactly pinpoint the subject. I suppose they're used to a more exact science." Lee again chuckled into the receiver. "They seem to have spent quite a lot of time—frankly—going around in circles."

"I'm sorry to hear that. Perhaps I could—"

"What I would like to ask you to do, if you're willing, is to collect some pertinent readings on this whole subject and put them in the reserve book room for the Club. We will be having our debate a week from Thursday—on the twentieth—so we wouldn't be tying up anything for too long a period."

"Of course. I'd be more than happy to do that for you. I'll have the librarian in charge of reserves set aside a shelf for the Club, and I'll put, say, fifteen or twenty books and articles on the shelf that they can consult. Does that sound all right?"

"That's splendid, Mr. Burt."

■ If you were Burt, which books and articles would you place on reserve for the Club? Evaluate Burt's list of sources which he suggested to the boys at the beginning of the case. For example, did he point out the best sources for the information required? What other sources could he have mentioned? Should he have offered to explain how to use the *ABS Guide,* a complicated bibliographic tool?

How would you assess Burt's attitude toward the social sciences? What does he mean when he says that social scientists have resolved the question of how scientific? What conclusions have you reached concerning this question—is there really a science of man? Is the jargon problem as bad as Lee suggests it is?

2

A Bit Of Unpleasantness At Amity

Amity City's fame derives more, perhaps, from Cortes Cola, which is bottled in the city, than from any other single source, the slogan "Cortes—The Cola That Makes Amity Friendly" being well-known throughout several far-western states. A thriving city of more than 650,000 people, who are, probably, no more friendly than people anywhere else, Amity has increased its population at an enormous rate during the past ten years. Last year, for example, Amity's Chamber of Commerce estimated that the city grew by 47 new residents each and every day. The environs of Amity, too, are growing rapidly—the most recent U.S. census figures place the population of the Amity metropolitan area at nearly one million.

Two years ago, a luxurious new central public library was constructed in midtown Amity, replacing a much less spacious and less auspiciously situated building which had served as the Amity Central Public Library since the early 1940's. When the library moved into its new quarters, Eric Harley, director of the library, introduced a number of significant changes in the library's operational procedures, including: 1) the closing of several branch libraries and replacing them with regular incity bookmobile service; 2) a changeover from Dewey Decimal to Library of Congress classification, complete with detailed plans for retrospective re-classification of the entire collection over a four year period; and 3) the introduction of subject departmentalization of reference services.

An aggressive library administrator who strongly believes that the average person rarely takes full advantage of the public library's service potential, Harley was confident that these organizational changes would

enable the Amity Public Library to serve the community more efficiently in the years ahead, thereby gradually enhancing the library's
reputation as an effective service institution. Also, at every available
opportunity, he proselytized for his belief that the community at large
should demand more and more in the way of service from its public
library, and not look upon it merely as a "lending station." In connection with National Library Week this past spring, Harley contributed
an article to the *Amity Argus Sunday Supplement* which set forth the
library's basic philosophy in these words:

> The tradition of the public library in America is one of *service*. Serv-
> ice to us here at the Amity Public Library means more than just the
> loaning of books, important as that service may be. The function of
> supplying quick, efficient, accurate information on any subject, either
> in person or via telephone, is also part and parcel of our service. By
> way of example, during this past month the Central Library success-
> fully answered such varied questions as: How many Eskimos live in
> Alaska? How to copyright a book? How many novels did the author
> B. Traven write and the titles of each? Are any courses in karate
> offered in Amity?
>
> Other services your Public Library offers include the locating and
> borrowing of books the Amity Public Library does not own; advice
> and help in choosing books on any subject you wish to explore; com-
> piling lists of books and other materials, such as films, on any sub-
> ject, except for students; and use of library facilities for public or
> private meetings of an educational nature.
>
> Your Public Library sums up its philosophy in one word: SERV-
> ICE. Can we serve you soon? We hope so!

During Eric Harley's six years as director of the Amity Public Library,
he has been successful in attracting a number of capable young librarians to his staff. Quite naturally, the professionals Harley has
brought to Amity share his service-oriented approach to public librarianship. One of these librarians, Charles Reedy, an imaginative and intellectually prepossessing man of 35, was appointed coordinator of the
social science division when subject departments were created. Reedy,
who possesses a master's degree in political science as well as in library
service, has done an impressive job over the past two years overseeing the development of the four departments which make up the social
science division. These departments are history and genealogy; political

science and government documents; business and economics; and sociology, education, and psychology. Responsible for book selection and specialized reference work within their respective areas, each department is ordinarily staffed with two professional librarians, a library intern who participates in Amity Public's work-study program, and one or two nonprofessionals.

Returning from her afternoon coffee break, Irene Schiller resumed her position at the reference desk in the sociology, education, and psychology department. "Sorry I'm a little late getting back, Mr. Itasca. It was terribly crowded in the lounge this afternoon." Louis Itasca, department head of SEP, as it was known, replied that those things happened occasionally and retired to his small office, a glass enclosed affair which allowed him to survey the reference and study area. Although the day had been exceptionally busy for a Tuesday, only a few people were now seated at the reading tables. Miss Schiller took up several reviewing journals and began reading. Her designated area for selection was education, although Itasca also kept an eye on new publications in the field since Miss Schiller had not yet completed her library degree and was officially classified as "sub-professional."

Miss Schiller became engrossed in a review of the latest book critical of the American high school, when a man's voice interrupted her.

"I'm sorry to bother you, mam, but the lady out there in the other room said you might be able to help me in here."

"That's perfectly all right. I'm here to help." Miss Schiller closed the periodical she was reading and motioned to the man to sit down. "Please sit down."

"My name's Thomas—Tom—Redman, and I'm—well—starting to write a book. And not too confidently, I should add."

"That's very interesting, Mr. Redman. A live author-to-be. My goodness."

"Really it's to be an anthology, with just an introduction by me. See, I'm something of a free-lance author in my spare time. I don't know if you've seen the new magazine Conservative Crusade or not, but I had an article published in it—in the first issue."

"No, I'm sorry, but I'm not familiar with that periodical."

"Well, to make a long story short, because of my article on the Nigra, Billy Joe Shaw, the publisher of Conservative Crusade, has asked me to do an anthology on the subject. See, Billy Joe wants to expand into book publishing."

"I see, yes."

"And since I've been told that you're willing to help people in my situation, I was hoping you'd help me find some books and things—about the Nigra. A bibliography of works, sort of."

"You've come to the right place, Mr. Redman. There are, fortunately, a number of good, recent bibliographies out on the Negro. And, of course, the library's catalog will list a good bit of material, too. Just what aspect are you going to deal with? I mean, are you limiting your anthology to contemporary problems or what?"

"Well, Mr. Shaw—Billy Joe—sees this as sort of a companion volume to Carleton Coon's *Origin of Races* and his other, more recent book—*The Living Races of Man.*"

"A companion volume to Coon's books?"

"That's right. You see, mam, Coon's pretty conclusive in his evidence but Billy Joe wants to bring together into one book other material which reaches the same conclusions as Coon does—other scientific evidence. I've read a lot of the recent things, and some of the classic works, like De Gobineau, but—"

"De Gobineau?"

"His *Essay on the Inequality of Races.* Actually, it's a lengthy treatise."

"I never heard of that essay—or treatise, Mr. Redman, but it sounds from the title like so much bigotry to me. The races, I assure you, are quite equal."

"It's a very scientific study of race done in the nineteenth century by a respected race scientist, I assure *you,* mam. Like Coon, De Gobineau puts the question of race in its proper perspective, showing the Caucasoid—or Caucasian, whichever you prefer—to be, shall I say, the most advanced race." Mr. Redman smiled slightly, showing a row of tobacco-stained teeth.

"We have no books like that in our library. We don't discriminate here. All books are carefully reviewed and we'd *never* buy anything that suggested a bigoted point of view. I'm afraid we can't help you with such a request." Miss Schiller's voice rose several decibels as she struggled to control her temper.

"Now wait one minute, mam. Bigotry is a bigoted word. You have Coon's books here—right? Coon shows the Caucasoid race is superior—right? All I want is help in finding other scientific books and essays like that. I'm not asking you to agree even if the eviden—"

"I *am* sorry, Mr.—Mr. Red—whatever your name is—BUT I don't want to pursue this. You'll get NO HELP from ME, I assure you. Now, I SUGGEST that you go before I—."

"Is there anything wrong here, Miss Schiller?" Louis Itasca had emerged from his office and was facing Miss Schiller and Redman.

"I was just explaining to this young woman," Redman began, "that I need some help about a research matter and she started shouting at me like I was an animal or something."

After some considerable effort, Itasca pieced together both versions of the unpleasant encounter. Finally, after suggesting that Miss Schiller, who was flushed and shaken, calm down in his office, Itasca turned to Redman. "May I have your full name, Mr. Redman, and telephone number? We'll give your request every attention. And when we've had time to compile a preliminary list—you want articles as well as books, don't you?"

"That's right. Articles, pamphlets, that kind of thing. The more I can see the better—for this kind of book."

"When we've compiled the list, we'll give you a call. Good day, Mr. Redman."

Later, after Miss Schiller had recovered her composure, Itasca explained that the library's function is to serve each patron as best it can, regardless of whether or not the patron's request is palatable to individual librarians. "A lawyer can choose his clients, Miss Schiller. Unfortunately, perhaps, the public librarian can't."

■ Assuming that the Amity Public Library's reference resources are adequate, what bibliographic tools should Itasca, who presumably will work on Redman's request, search in order to locate materials which scientifically treat the question of racial superiority and/or inferiority? Comment on Miss Schiller's assertion that "fortunately, a number of good, recent bibliographies . . . on the Negro" are available. Consider, too, her statement that "we'd *never* buy anything that suggested a bigoted point of view."

3

It All Began With Abner Doubleday

C.B. Hennandoah
5 Pine Terrace
Redlands Heights,
California
April 14, 19—

Doncaster College
Library
Pequot, Missouri

Gentlemen:

Many years ago I became interested in pursuing the study of history. Local library facilities were inadequate for my purpose. To limit long trips to these institutions, I decided to form a history collection for my personal use. It has been my aim to acquire one or more books covering almost all phases of history. As a result, my collection now contains 6,143 volumes, requiring approximately 650 feet of shelf space.

Because of the size of my collection, I became interested in the science of classification. I decided to use the Dewey Decimal Classification system, in connection with the Cutter-Sanborn Three-figure Author Table. My collection is completely classified and indexed by Isabel S. Monro's *Sears List of Subject Headings*. My catalogue contains approximately 20,000 3" x 5" cards of the best physical quality.

At my present age (79), the time is coming when I must seek a depository for my history books. The collection is *not for sale*. I have always hoped that some day I could give the collection to a library where it would be useful in the pursuit of knowledge. I have chosen to write

11

to Doncaster College because for many years I have admired the consistent quality of the College baseball team. Many persons avidly follow major league baseball, as I do, but few interest themselves in minor league or college aspects of the sport. Next to the study of history, baseball is my greatest pleasure. While I have never seen the Doncaster College nine play, I carefully follow the finest teams in the country. Overall, Doncaster College has the best record for the past five years.

To replace my collection at current prices of older books would amount to a great deal of money. I believe its worth to be approximately $40,000 and I would require a statement of value to that effect. I do not wish to have my collection "broken up" by heirs who have no knowledge of books and their worth. My great-grandson, Arnold Hennandoah, is at present in the military service of his country. As is the case with so many young men today, he has exhibited little or no interest in intellectual pursuits. Should Doncaster College be interested in my collection, it must remain intact and not dismembered in any way. Because of the wide field of knowledge covered, it is an ideal collection as it exists. Shipping charges would rest with the library.

I shall be happy to correspond with you if Doncaster College is interested in adding my history collection of 6,143 volumes to its library. I am,

Yours sincerely,

Caleb B. Hennandoah

DONCASTER COLLEGE

Craig Library

40-42 Arrow Street

Pequot, Missouri

George A. Mercer, Director   April 27, 19—

Mr. Caleb B. Hennandoah
5 Pine Terrace
Redlands Heights, California

Dear Mr. Hennandoah:

In reply to your most kind letter of April 14, allow me to say that the Craig Library is very much interested in your gracious offer to donate a history collection of some 6,000 volumes to the Library's growing collections, which are approaching the 90,000 volume mark with this year's accessions. As such, I am sure that you will be gratified to know that the Craig Library is the intellectual center of the College.

Your letter does raise several questions in my mind. Would it be possible for us here at the Library to know more specifically about the nature of the contents of your collection? This information would help us immeasurably in ascertaining if your books would be useful additions to the Craig's collections. Another question which occurs to me concerns the breaking up of your collection. I gather, from the tenor of your remarks, that you are particularly eager to keep the collection together as a unit. I would point out that, should the College accept your generous offer, it would be very beneficial for the Library if your collection could be integrated into our basic undergraduate collection.

Once again, Mr. Hennandoah, allow me to express my gratitude on behalf of the College and the Craig Library for thinking of us here at Doncaster. I am enclosing a recent photograph of the Craig Library, a fine old building which is maintained by a fine staff of well-trained librarians.

I should add that the Doncaster team, as you undoubtedly know, is off to another splendid start this season.

I will look forward to hearing from you in the near future.

Sincerely yours,

George A. Mercer.
Director

GAM:jm
Encl.

C.B. Hennandoah
5 Pine Terrace
Redlands Heights,
California
June 2, 19—

Dr. G.A. Mercer
Director, Craig Library
Doncaster College
40-42 Arrow Street
Pequot, Mo.

Dear Dr. Mercer:

All my life I have favored the "New" historians over their narrower brethren. I am a disciple of James Harvey Robinson and my collection shows history in its widest application. Useful as it was, I found gratification when the old *Cambridge Modern History* was replaced with the *New Modern History*. I feel certain that Lord Acton would have been pleased.

My secretary has compiled a list of the books in my collection. To give all the details would have made the task for her too arduous. Needless to say, you will recognize the books as standard works in the field of history. You will also see that I have added little to my collection since the 1950's due to poor health. Meticulous in all she attempts, my secretary is not beyond error. I wish to point out that I have been unable to carefully examine the enclosed list. My eyesight has served me remarkably well for 79 years, but it is no longer up to sustained reading.

My collection must *not* be dismembered or "integrated" if I am to entrust it to your college. It was chosen to cover all phases of history and is an ideal reference collection as it stands. As mentioned previously, I used Melvil Dewey's wondrous Decimal Classification system (twelfth edition). In this way, all my books stand in relation to each other and can be utilized as a whole.

It pleases me that Doncaster College is interested in adding my collection to its library. Upon receipt of your further instructions, I shall have the collection prepared for shipment.

Thank you for the photograph of the library. I remain,

Yours sincerely,

Caleb B. Hennandoah

After receiving Mr. Hennandoah's second letter and the list of books comprising his collection (*see* Appendix), George Mercer turned the project over to James Schuyler, Doncaster's reference librarian.

"We're weak—very weak—in history, Jim, as you know, and when I received this old fellow's original letter I thought it might be worth a postage stamp to investigate. I never dreamed he'd go to all the trouble of having a list typed. My God—over 6,000 entries! What I'd like you to do, Jim, is check and see which titles we already have and then determine if we can use much of the other stuff. Unfortunately, as you'll see when you've had a chance to read the correspondence I've had with old Hennandoah, we have to accept this collection *en bloc* or not at all. If you decide we can use the collection, I'll put it in the stacks, down by the old newspapers, at least for the time being. Give his list a thorough going-over. Six thousand books at one fell swoop would look pretty nice in the annual report. On the other hand, I don't want to acquire it just to clutter up the stacks with a lot of junk. God knows, if his comments about the Cambridge histories are any indication, he doesn't know a tinker's damn about history."

"Are you going to ask the history department to look over the list?"

"At this juncture? No, Jim, I don't think so. This *could* be a real coup for the library and I don't want Howes and his boys getting mixed up in this thing just yet. If you decide it's worth taking, I'll present Howes with a *fait accompli*, then see the president and tell him how wonderful we are in the library. Besides, you have some background in history, don't you?"

"I minored in it in college. I know Schlesinger senior from junior, but that's about it."

"Don't let that worry you, Jim. Our job's book evaluation and, by God, we've got to evaluate now."

Doncaster College, a private liberal arts college, is best known in Missouri and surrounding states for its teacher education program, especially its physical education curriculum. Undergraduate enrollment currently stands at 1,381 students. Increasingly, principals and teachers in secondary and elementary schools are being attracted to Doncaster's advanced program in education which leads to the degrees of master of arts or master of education. At the present time, the graduate school has close to 175 students, most of whom study at Doncaster on a part time basis. The history department at Doncaster is a lackluster affair at best, unable to retain its good young teachers and, conversely, unable to expunge its deadwood. The department offers some twenty courses, all on the undergraduate level, which range from required courses such as United States History (two semesters), History of Civilization (also two semesters), Missouri History, and Recent World Problems to electives such as Economic History of the United States, History of Russia, History of England, Early European History, and Modern European History.

Craig Library itself can hardly be considered a librarian's paradise. With a collection of 85,000 volumes which is growing by only approximately 3,500 volumes a year, the library is top-heavy with materials reflecting the education department's programs. Much of the library problem at Doncaster centers on the fact that Mercer receives only a bare two percent of the College's general operating budget. The initially low book fund is further emasculated by the demands made on it by the education department, the most prestigious unit at Doncaster. Shortage of funds is also responsible for the lack of adequate professional and clerical staff at the Craig Library. The reference department, for example, is unable to offer service in the evenings or on the weekends for this reason, and the technical services department has only one professional cataloger. George Mercer is fully aware of these problems, but he has been powerless during his seven years as director of the library to correct them.

■ What recommendations should Schuyler make to Mercer concerning the Hennandoah collection, after considering such determinants as 1) How valuable will this collection be to the history department and its curriculum? 2) Is the collection comprised of "standard works in the field of history" as Hennandoah claims? 3) Assuming that Doncaster uses Dewey as its classification system, what problems would the acquisition of the collection pose for what is a small cataloging department? Comment also on Hennandoah's claim to be a devotee of the "New History."

Appendix

Bibliography of the Hennandoah History Collection, A-An

Aaron, D., *Men of Good Hope.* 1951
Aaronovitch, S. *Crisis in Kenya.* 1947
Abailard, P. *Historia Calamitatum.* 1922
Abbott, C. *Australia's Frontier Province.* 1950
Abbott, F.F. *Common People of Rome.* 1911
Abbott, G.F. *Thucydides.* 1925
Abbott, W. *Expansion of Europe.* 1924 (one v. ed.)
Abegg, L. *Mind of East Asia.* 1952
Abel, T. *Why Hitler Came to Power.* 1938
Abel, W. *Die Wustungen Des Ausgehenden Mitte Lalters.* 1955
   (2d ed.)
Abell, A. *Urban Impact of American Protestantism.* 1865-1900. 1943
Abend, H. *My Life in China.* 1943
Aberle, D.F. *Kinship System of the Kalmuk Mongols.* 1953
*Abernethy, T. *Western Lands and The American Revolution.* 1937

Asterisk (*) denotes titles on this list which are held by the Craig Library

Aboussouan, B. *Problème Politique Syrien.* 1925
Abraham, G.E.H. *Hundred Years of Music.* 1938
Abram, A. *English Life and Manners in the Later Middle Ages.* 1913
*Abram, A. *Social England in the Fifteenth Century.* 1909
Adams, A. *Log of a Cowboy.* 1903
Adams, E.D. *British Interests and Activities in Texas,* 1838-1846. 1915
Adams, E.D. *Great Britain and the American Civil War.* 1925 (2v.)
Adams, G.B. *Constitutional History of England.* 1921
Adams, G.B. *Council and Courts of Anglo-Norman England.* 1926
Adams, G.K. & Hutter. *Mad Forties.* 1942
*Adams, G.M. *Spain and Portugal.* 1906
*Adams, Henry B. *History of the United States.* 1889-91 (4v.; v.3 missing)
Adams, Henry B. & C.F. *Chapters of Erie.* 1871
Adams, Herbert B. *Seminary Notes on Historical Literature.* 1890.
Adams, J.Q. *Writings* (ed. by Ford). 1913-17 (7v.)
*Adams, J.T. *Album of American History.* 1944-49 (5v.)
*Adams, J.T. *Atlas of American History.* 1943
*Adams, J.T. *Dictionary of American History.* 1940 (6v.)
Adams, R.G. *History of the Foreign Policy of the US.* 1924
Adams, R.G. & Peckham. *Lexington to Fallen Timbers,* 1775-1794. 1942
Adamov, E.A. *Konstantinopol I Prolivy.* 1925-26 (2v.)
*Addams, J. *Twenty Years at Hull-House.* 1910
Addams, J. *The Second Twenty Years.* 1930
Adler, C. & Margalith. *With Firmness in the Right.* 1946
Adock, F. & Whibley. *Constitutions.* 1916 (3d ed.)
Agabekov, G. *Russian Secret Terror.* 1931
Agar, H. *Price of Union.* 1950
Airy, O. *Charles II.* 1904
Airy, O. *English Restoration and Louis XIV.* 1879
Aiyangar, S. *Ancient India.* 1911
Albion, R. *Forests and Sea Power.* 1926
Albright, W. *From the Stone Age to Christianity.* 1940
*Alden, J.R. *American Revolution.* 1954
Aleksandrov, G. *Pattern of Soviet Democracy.* 1948
Alexander, B. *Last Journey.* 1912
Ali, A. *Making of India.* 1925
Alington, C. *Europe.* 1948
Alington, C. *Growth of the US.* 1938
Allen, A. *History of Verona.* 1910
*Allen, F. *The Big Change.* 1952
Allen, J.H. *Unitarian Movement Since the Reformation.* 1895
Allen, J.W. *History of Political Thought in the Sixteenth Century.* 1928
*Allen, P. *Age of Erasmus.* 1914
Allen, W. & Muratoff. *Russian Campaigns of 1941-1943.* 1944
Allen, W. & Muratoff. *Russian Campaigns of 1944-1945.* 1946
*Almond, G. *The American People and Foreign Policy.* 1950

Alvarez, A. *Monroe Doctrine.* 1924
American Heritage. *Golden Book of America.*1957
*American Historical Association. *Guide to Historical Literature.* 1931
*American Historical Association. *Guide to Historical Literature.* 1961
Ames, M. *America, Heir of Yesterday.* 1948
Amet, J. *Le Jutland.* 1923
Anchel, R. *Napoleon et les Juifs.* 1928
Anderson, Adelaide. *Humanity and Labour in China.* 1928
Anderson, A.T. *Sweden in the Baltic.* 1947
Anderson, B. *Farmer Seeks Jeffersonian Democracy.* 1943
Anderson, F. *Constitutions . . . of France, 1789-1909.* 1909 (2d ed.)
Anderson, G. & Subedar. *Expansion of British India, 1818-1858.* 1918
Anderson, H & Lindquist. *Selected Test Items in World History.* 1938
Andersson, J. *Researches into the Prehistory of the Chinese.* 1945
Andrews, C. *Colonial Period in American History.* 1934-38. (4v.)
Andrus, J. *Burmese Economic Life.* 1948
Anthony, I. *Raleigh and His World.* 1934
Anthony, J. *Birth of the US.* 1938
Anthony, K. *Catherine the Great.* 1927
Antsigerov, A. *Russian Agriculture During the War.* 1930

4

Psychic Phenomena

Florence Smith often commented to her friends that she wanted to die with her boots on. Unlike most people who have this desire, Miss Smith was succinctly obliged one afternoon in her office, and at the funeral her friends, though properly agonized with grief, could not help saying to one another how fortunate Flo had been to die with her boots on, just as she had wished. Miss Smith's death, however, was not viewed with such equanimity by members of the Mount Ida Public Library's board of trustees, who now had to find a new town librarian—and quickly, too, since the remodeling project was scheduled to begin in only three months.

Mount Ida is a reasonably pleasant, self-contained, steady community —*The World Almanac* shows that its population increased slightly from 21,009 to 24,874 in the last decade—with just enough light industry for the local League of Women Voters to be concerned with environmental pollution. The nearest large city, Shirley, located forty miles north of Mount Ida, is easily accessible by a four-lane highway, constructed in the mid-1960's as part of the federal road building program. While most Mount Idans are a bit snobbish or defensive about Shirley—a dirty, ugly, sooty, corrupt, etcetera place, they say—an increasing number of young married couples have taken to buying their clothing and furniture there, a practice which has offended the strong local mercantile sensibilities of the older generation. In a town where local initiative and self-sufficiency are valued, where family tradition and names such as Bothwell and Swan mean something, where the solidarity and respectability of the past seem threatened by modern attitudes, such acts as "dealing in Shirley" are construed as vulgar, disloyal, and even heretical.

When Flo Smith died, a number of people in town looked upon Miss

Jenny Tucker as the logical person to accede to the position of library director. Miss Tucker, after all, had been an able assistant director in charge of public services for ten or eleven years, she was a local woman, and, no doubt about it, she knew her books. Weighed against the facts that she was a bit odd, and that she did not have a library degree as such, Miss Tucker still seemed like a fine choice. However, Blake Bothwell, chairman of the board of trustees, was determined to see a man appointed as librarian. His arguments impressed his fellow board members mightily: a man naturally has a better business head than a woman, and with the remodeling expenditures and the larger operating budget voted for the next fiscal year, a better business head was most desirable; a man could better deal with the sassy teenagers who used the library as a hangout during the winter; and, besides, Salford, a neighboring town of 13,000 enterprising citizens, had a male librarian. Bothwell did not bother to mention that he intensely disliked Miss Jenny Tucker—he did not have to, since everyone on the board knew it.

Blake Bothwell rarely tried to get what he knew he could not get, and, therefore, two months after Flo Smith had been laid to rest, a thin young man with an intelligent face named Edgar Pine was hired as town librarian. Pine, who had been a cataloger at the Shirley Public Library, a fact which caused Bothwell and the board some uneasiness, was candid with Mr. Bothwell when he applied for the directorship, telling him that he viewed the Mount Ida position as a steppingstone to bigger and better things administratively. Bothwell said that he admired ambition in a young man, and that if Pine could see his way clear to stay at Mount Ida for at least two or three years, the job was his. Pine agreed to this condition and, after the formalities of being hired were completed, promptly settled into his new job. Some people, of course, were distressed and irritated that Miss Jenny Tucker's application had not received favorable consideration by the board, but this feeling soon disappeared, at least in most quarters.

One of the major reasons that resentment toward Pine failed to materialize was his popular idea to allow adult patrons of the library to "Borrow a Bushel of Books" before the remodeling project began. The invitation not only appealed to library users but, as Pine explained to his staff, "the more books people have at home during the remodeling, the fewer we'll have to move around." Because the extensive remodeling necessitated closing the main adult fiction and nonfiction collections for two months, with only a small rental collection and the children's room left in operation, the inventiveness of Pine's idea was counted as a stroke of genius.

One morning, several days before the remodeling project was about to begin, Pine asked Miss Jenny Tucker to come to his office.

"You wished to see me?"

"Yes, Miss Tucker. Please sit down. I wanted to see you because you probably won't have too much to do for the next two months—until the remodeling is over."

"I'm sure you will understand when I say that my department has quite a number of matters which need attending to." Miss Tucker supervised three ladies who worked at the circulation desk, handled any reference questions which were received, and made certain that the high school students who worked as pages did not loaf on the job.

"Well, Mrs. Carmel and Mrs. Foster won't be working during the remodeling, and Miss Pratt is going to be in the children's room most of the time. And you won't have the pages to worry with."

"I *mean* that I will have quite a bit to do." Miss Tucker tried to control her annoyance with Pine, whom she called—in private—a "young pup."

"I'm certain you'll be able to put the free time to good use. What I want—hope you'll be able to do is devote some time during the remodeling to book selection. In July, as you know, the budget will be increased, and the remodeling will give us space for about 20,000 more books—counting the compact storage unit." Currently, the library has 57,000 volumes. "So this will be a good time to think about filling in some gaps in the collection by, ah, checking the *Standard Catalog for Public Libraries* and other standard lists."

"I have *already* started a special selection project." Miss Tucker saw a frown begin to form on Pine's face. "I anticipated that you may want me to do something like that."

"What kind of *special* project?" Pine was suspicious and his voice showed it.

"Selecting books on psychic phenomena, for one thing."

"What?—E.S.P. and that sort of thing?"

"I know you have not yet had the opportunity to completely get to know Mount Ida, but *when* you do, you will find a great interest here in psychic phenomena."

"You mean E.S.P. and clairvoyance?"

"Clairvoyance, telepathy, precognition, extrasensory perception, accelerated plant growth—psychic phenomena."

Pine began to chuckle. "*You* don't mean to tell me that you actually believe in that nonsense, do you, Miss Tucker?"

"I did *not* say, Mr. Pine, that I believed in psychic phenomena. However, it is certainly worthy of close study." Miss Tucker restrained herself admirably.

"Do you actually think that a public library ought to spend money on that kind of thing?"

"Mr. Pine. Anything that is of interest to our community *ought* to be purchased. I might add, for your information, that there is sufficient evidence that most of us have latent extrasensory perception. The obvious fact is that human beings have not completed their development." When Pine made no immediate effort to reply to this ringing statement, Miss Tucker continued. "I have even myself talked to flowers—and they grew and prospered. It's a matter of developing one's dormant psychic abilities."

Pine tried to keep a straight face. "Tell me, what books do we have in the library on this psychic phenomena business?"

"Very, very few. Flo—Miss Smith—was narrow-minded about the subject. I had her read the excellent *World of Ted Serios*, but she could never make the necessary effort required to overcome her prejudices."

"Well, Miss Tucker, I don't know much about the subject either. I had a ouija board when I was little, but that's about it. But I do know that we can't cater to every—every pseudoscientific cult that comes along. I guess some people still believe in werewolves and voodoo or that calories don't count, but I can't see any merit in putting loads of books in the library on these subjects. There are too many important subjects around."

"This discussion is beginning to tense me up, Mr. Pine. Psychic research *is* one of the most important subjects in the world today. Someday even people like you will have to admit it." Miss Tucker looked very white, and hands shook as she spoke.

"I'm sorry, Miss Tucker. I really didn't mean to upset you. All right. Why don't you let me have a list of books on this psychic phenomena business that you think we ought to buy—*with* a list of those we already have. Then I'll decide if we want any of them. How's that? Now—let's talk about checking the *Standard Catalog* against our collection."

After concluding this rather unhappy conference with Miss Tucker, Pine could not help wondering if Miss Smith, his predecessor, had succumbed, not to a heart attack, but rather to pins stuck into a little doll by a woman who talked to flowers?

■ Comment on Pine's attitude toward psychic phenomena. What is the current state of research in parapsychology? Should the public library purchase materials in this area? If so, what books would you recommend for the Mount Ida Public Library?

5

Bibliographies And Banana Mountains

Richard Douglas Pomeroy, librarian at Kinross State College, was feeling much better than he had the previous day. So much better, he confided to Thelma Tunneman, his reference librarian, who was having lunch with him, that he was about to throw caution to the wind and order a "banana mountain" for dessert. Yes, he was feeling much better today.

"Trains," Pomeroy told Miss Tunneman, "always joggle my weight around, and after a long trip I feel slightly top-heavy. My wife says I ought to diet—she even wants to use some kind of dietary sour cream! I will say this, though—the next time I go to Midwinter, I'm going to fly. If the plane'll hold me, that is." Pomeroy, who weighed well over 250 pounds, enjoyed making small jokes about his large figure.

"I've never gone to a midwinter convention." Miss Tunneman carefully replaced her cup in its saucer. "I guess I'm like the old Brooklyn Dodgers who used to say, 'Wait'll next year.' I did get to a New York annual meeting of ALA once, but that was eons ago. As I remember, it was quite educational."

"Thelma, you'll have to go out with me next year. Be on the Coast, I think. National professional meetings help me keep up with developments in the field. And, believe me, since I've become involved in this building program, I need something to help me keep up. You know, some months I don't even get through *LJ*."

"Well, that's something I *do* manage to do."

"Speaking of keeping up reminds me. Thelma, what's your opinion of these Universal Reference Service bibliographies? Joe Sever, the young fellow out at Joiner College—you may know him—was telling me in Chicago how valuable they are. Don't ask me how Joe and I got on that subject."

"I think it's Universal Reference *System*."

"That's right—System. I remember you had spoken to me about it once a long time ago, and I couldn't for the life of me remember when I was talking to Joe what conclusions you'd come to about it. Inform me." Pomeroy smiled across the table as he scooped into his banana mountain.

"Well, when the first volume of ten or twelve in political science was published—in 1965 or 1966, I believe—I received some promotional literature about this URS and, as closely as I can remember, there were a number of reasons why I decided not to order it."

"You didn't buy it? Now that *is* interesting. Joe spent the good part of an hour at breakfast Friday morning bending my ear about how wonderful this whole URS plan is. He seems to think it's the greatest thing that's happened in social science bibliography since the UNESCO series. They're done by computers, I think he said?"

"URS? I believe so. But I'm not positive, Mr. Pomeroy. I do remember that the bibliographies in the series have some funny arrangement. Yes —that's right! They're arranged by *author* entry. That's one reason why I decided against getting any of them."

"Arranged by *author*? That's a bit strange, isn't it?"

"That's what I thought. All the bibliographies of that kind, like *PAIS* and the UNESCO bibliographies—and *Foreign Affairs Bibliography* for that matter—are arranged in some classified manner."

"You're sure about that? URS, I mean."

"Pretty positive. Because—I remember now—the URS bibliographies have a lot of complicated symbols to compensate for their author arrangement. Some kind of new subject index, I think."

"Well I wonder why Joe—?"

"I think, too, Mr. Pomeroy, that the reviews were not too favorable at the time. In fact, the same man—I forget his name—who's in charge of URS published that *ABS Guide to Social Science Literature* which was not recommended by the Subscription Books Committee. Remember, we talked about it when it came out—in 1965, too, I think. I can't remember offhand if URS bibliographies have been reviewed in *Subscription Books Bulletin* or not."

"Well—that was *some* banana mountain!"

"Was it good?"

"Umm-m-m. Let's see—where were we? Oh yes, URS. Thelma, why don't you, just to be on the safe side, reevaluate these URS bibliographies. No hurry, but perhaps we ought to reconsider them. Sever was *very* impressed. What do you say?"

"Probably be a good idea, Mr. Pomeroy. It can't hurt. I'll look into it and give you a full report."

Kinross is a thriving little town of 14,000 population, located approximately sixty miles south of Hagar, a prominent industrial city of well over two million. The general bulletin of the State College at Kinross characterizes the community as "having diversified light industry, a strong sense of church and religion, and a great pride in the College." Founded as a normal school in the early part of this century, Kinross State became a state teachers college in 1935, and, in 1961, it acheived status as a state college as a result of adding programs which lead to the bachelor of arts degree. Today, Kinross State College enrolls somewhere in the neighborhood of 1,400 undergraduate students, twice the number enrolled just a decade ago. Moreover, nearly 250 graduate students are currently engaged in study leading to the master of science degree in education. The majority of these graduate students are studying on a part-time basis.

The Samuel H. Breeds Library, named in honor of a former governor who achieved certain distinction among educators by actively promoting an improved system of public higher education in the state, was built eight years ago. Breeds Library, designed for a capacity of 70,000 volumes, is a striking building of modified Gothic design constructed of Berea sandstone. Because of the college's rapid expansion during the last eight years, the Breeds Library has long been inadequate in terms of space to house expanding collections. Consequently, a sizable addition to the existing building which will double the present stack area is currently being planned. The administration, including Pomeroy, is hopeful that the addition will be completed within the next year.

The library's reference collection, naturally strong in the field of education, contains most of the sources listed in the Enoch Pratt Free Library publication, *Reference Books*, with the exception of several expensive tools such as *Chemical Abstracts* and the British Museum's *General Catalogue of Printed Books*. Except for the *London Bibliography of the Social Sciences*, Breeds Library holds the important general bibliographic sources in the social and behavioral sciences.

■ If you were Miss Tunneman, how would you evaluate the basic plan of the Universal Reference System? What comments would you make concerning the usefulness of URS's "Political Science, Government, and Public Policy Series" as compared with *Foreign Affairs Bibliography? International Political Science Abstracts?* UNESCO's *International Bibliography of the Social Sciences: Political Science?* Public Affairs Information Service, *Bulletin? London Bibliography of the Social Sciences?* What is your opinion of Miss Tunneman's "offhand" appraisal of URS? Of the *ABS Guide to Recent Publications in the Social and Behavioral Sciences?* In your opinion, considering what you know about Kinross State College, should Miss Tunneman reverse her earlier decision and purchase the URS bibliographies?

6

Vanity Fair

"Perhaps this will help put the situation in some perspective for you, Mr. Payne." Taylor Marston, director of the Gustine Memorial Public Library at Myrtlebank, pushed a mounted newspaper clipping across his desk to Gerald Payne, who was being interviewed for the position of reference librarian. "While you're looking over that, I'll get us some coffee. Or would you prefer tea?"

"Thank you, no. Coffee will be fine." Payne began to concentrate on the news item.

MYRTLEBANK RECEIVES $600,000 LIBRARY FROM HEIRESS
By Mervin Paxton

A charming benefactress is primarily responsible for the handsome new $600,000 public library in Myrtlebank. She is Leonora Gustine, daughter of the late John R. Gustine, who is remembered as "the millionaire cyclist" because he frequently rode to his Wall Street office on a bicycle.

Dedicated yesterday with many prominent Myrtlebank residents attending, the Gustine Memorial Public Library is an attractive, spacious one-story structure of contemporary architectural design. The library's graceful interior has a restful courtyard with comfortable benches and a large elm tree in the center. Reading areas are exquisitely furnished with easy chairs, modernistic bookracks, and thick carpets.

Miss Gustine, who participated in the lavish dedication ceremonies, told of her father's strong belief that education is Democracy's greatest bulwark against the spread of the world communist conspiracy. "He would strongly approve of my gift were he here," said Miss Gustine.

C.C. Short, Mayor of the residential Myrtlebank community of 12,000, revealed that he had originally approached Miss Gustine two years ago for a contribution to the proposed new library building. "Hoping to keep the tax rate down and avoid a bond issue fight, I sought private donations. After seeing the building plans, Miss Gustine pledged $400,000 for the building and furnishings. At first I was flabbergasted, but now the idea doesn't seem a bit strange. The whole town is very grateful to her," Mayor Short said. In addition to her $400,000 largess, Miss Gustine has given $50,000 to be used to establish and maintain a genealogy collection in the library.

As Miss Gustine's generosity became known, other gifts were received by the library. Outstanding among these is the Ellen Logan Hartwell Phono-listening Room, given by Joseph P. Hartwell in memory of his wife, a former library trustee and President of the Myrtlebank League of Women Voters.

The librarian, Taylor N. Marston, said that the library now has 31,000 volumes. The new library will hold up to 75,000 volumes. Says Mr. Marston, "Over the last five years, the old library was terribly crowded. Now we will be able to give Myrtlebank the kind of library service a community of this kind deserves."

The new Gustine Memorial Library is adjacent to the municipal parking lot on Arcadia Parkway.

"You see, Mr. Payne, the problem is that we have never had a proper reference librarian. Before we moved into these quarters, the staff always dealt with questions the best they could, with the more difficult ones passed on to me. Well, with the new building, I feel—and the trustees agree wholeheartedly—that now is the best time to alter this situation. Frankly, I don't have the time to devote to reference work that it requires, particularly since we moved. As you might expect, use of the library has increased tremendously over the past three months. Circulation has trebled, the lounges and study areas are almost always filled to capacity. And our book budget has increased, so that there's a heck of a lot of selecting to be done. It's quite encouraging, but a bit hectic right now."

"Has student use of the library increased much since you moved?"

"It certainly has. Before, we had a steady group of students who used the library, but now—well, I never realized Myrtlebank had so many children. Of course, I should add that Myrtlebank has a very fine school system, and both the junior high and high school libraries are excellent—but they're not open in the evenings or on weekends."

"I can see why you have decided to have a reference librarian. Students, I'm told, ask a lot of questions and need help in finding their way around the library."

"That's quite true, Mr. Payne. A heck of a lot of questions. They're a real challenge."

"What else would the reference librarian do? I mean besides answering questions."

"Helping with selection, of course. And our vertical file needs a professional hand. And, should you come to Myrtlebank, one of your first duties would be to build—rather quickly—a basic genealogy collection. We've been operating in the Gustine now for three months, and I haven't had the time to get to it. I think it's mentioned in the clipping you just read—" There was a knock on Marston's office door. "Excuse me, that's probably the coffee." After both men had completed the ritual of fixing their coffee, Marston continued talking about the genealogy collection. "As you read in the clipping, Miss Gustine also gave us $50,000 for a genealogy collection. Since she's getting along in years, I would like to have this collection ready for use as soon as possible. It means a great deal to her—Miss Gustine is very patriotic and she believes that knowledge of family descendants and lineage nourishes pride in our country. And I think, too, that because of her generosity to the library we owe it to her to get the collection started as soon as we can."

"I want to be honest with you, Mr. Marston. I've never worked with genealogical sources. In library school, we didn't do much with that area, outside of examining Burke's Peerage."

"I appreciate your candor, Mr. Payne, but I don't think this would present any real problem. Of course experience is always desirable, but we all have to start somewhere, don't we? And while the responsibility for a collection like this is a big one, there are guides—and with $50,000 a few minor mistakes now and then shouldn't hurt too much."

"Has the library done much with genealogy in the past? I mean, before you moved in here?"

"Very little, although the demand is there. We have a few standard sources. Burke's Peerage, which you mentioned. And several years ago we started getting the Rider *Index to American Genealogical Materials*. And, of course, we have the Virkus genealogical encyclopedia—the *Compendium*. And we recently bought a reprint copy of the Library of Congress bibliography, *American and English Genealogies*. Other than that, to my recollection, that's about it—except for a few local and county sources. Frankly, I think you would find the genealogical aspects of the job a real challenge. Now, Mr. Payne, how about a Cook's tour of the library? Then we can come back here and talk more specifically."

Marston, who had previously interviewed two other applicants for the reference position, was favorably impressed by Gerald Payne. He possessed a master's degree in library science, his military service obligation was completed, and he appeared to be well-mannered and poised for a young man. Thus, despite the fact that Payne had only recently graduated from library school and lacked professional experience, Marston decided that he would probably offer the reference job to Payne.

■ If Gerald Payne takes the Myrtlebank job, how should he proceed with starting a basic genealogy collection? What sources should he initially purchase? After the collection is established, what policy problems may arise? How are these problems usually handled? Is it realistic for a small public library to maintain a genealogy collection? Will $50,000 be adequate to finance such a collection?

7

The Professor And
The Plagiarist

"I *am* sorry, Dr. Goldie—I, I didn't see you *down* there."

"That's quite all right, Miss, ah—"

"Miss Kondazian. Is there *anything* I can help you with, Dr. Goldie?"

"I suppose I shouldn't be sprawled out like this, but it *is* upsetting to receive a plagiarized paper—I've been trying to track down the source."

"You mean the student *copied?*"

"This paper," replied the professor somewhat ruefully, "is obviously cribbed. From beginning to end—except perhaps for the final paragraph. And I'm trying—with scant luck so far—to locate the source the student used. I've already looked through the *American Economic Review* since 1961."

"That *is* a problem, Doctor. Maybe Mrs. Boyd could help. She's just marvelous at finding things—just like Sherlock Holmes. And I *just* bet—"

"Mrs. Boyd?"

"She's our reference librarian—you know."

"Oh yes—Mrs. *Boyd.* Sits at that desk upstairs sometimes."

"That's her. I'll just give her a buzz. Excuse me, Doctor, for just a second."

Within several minutes, Kay Boyd entered the Periodicals and Reserve Book Room. "I'm not scheduled at the desk at the moment, Shirley, so I came right down." Turning to Dr. Goldie, who was busily leafing through a bound volume of the *Harvard Business Review*, Mrs. Boyd smiled. "Good afternoon, Dr. Goldie. Miss Kondazian tells me you want to copy an article from the *American Economic Review*. We have—"

"No, not quite. You're Mrs. Boyd?"

"That's right. Don't you remember—we met formally at the President's Tea in September?"

"Of course—how silly of me. Of course. To answer your original question, I'm trying to locate the source a student used in a plagiarized paper. Here—look at this." Dr. Goldie handed her a dog-eared student paper (*see* Appendix I). "This paper is obviously plagiarized, and if I could find incontrovertible proof, I'd have the little cheater expelled. But I haven't had any luck so far. I've been through *AER*—maybe *HBR* will show up something."

Mrs. Boyd studied the paper as Dr. Goldie spoke. "This paper was written for 'Contemporary Economic Society'?"

"Yes. I have my students choose detailed subjects such as our balance of payments problem or price fluctuations in the retail market—or, as in this case, Latin American trade developments. And that paper in your hand is as blatant a piece of plagiarism as I've ever encountered. The student is not only not capable of that kind of analysis, but the prose is much too sophisticated. It was obviously written by an expert—a professor no doubt."

"And there's not a single footnote, either. If I were you, Dr. Goldie, I'd simply confront the girl and she'd probably confess on the spot."

"You must understand, Mrs. Bird, that I'm not a fanatic about footnotes."

"Mrs. *Boyd*."

"Of course—Mrs. *Boyd*. Sorry. I make it clear to my students that I don't want them spending all their time making beautiful footnotes. I want them to *think*. Under the circumstances, I can hardly upbraid her for not including footnotes."

"And she does have a short bibliography. Let's see. Victor Urquidi's— hope I'm pronouncing that correctly—Urquidi's *Free Trade and Economic Integration in Latin America*. John Lindeman's *Preferential Trading Systems in Latin America*. And two articles. One from *Inter-American Economic Affairs* and one in *Foreign Affairs*. That's not bad."

"I've checked all those references, and it's obvious that she was clever enough not to cite the source she plagiarized."

"But is her bibliography appropriate? I mean, do these books and articles apply to her paper?"

"Conceivably. Both Cochrane and Plaza's articles deal with the subject. And sections of Lindeman and Urquidi. This girl's *very* clever, make no mistake."

Appleton College, founded in 1927, is a coeducational, liberal arts college of over 800 undergraduate students. Tucked away in a remote section of one of the Northeastern states, Appleton draws most of its students from the regional area. Its growth has not been spectacular, but each year for the past decade or so the college has increased its student enrollment by twenty or thirty. Likewise, a new building manages to be constructed every three or four years.

From the date of its founding, Appleton has had, by its standards, a strong business and economics department. The fact that its first two presidents were businessmen-turned-educators had some influence on this development. During the past few years, the current president and the chairman of the business and economics department have worked to create the image of an undergraduate "Harvard Business School" at Appleton. While the results of this attempt have been minimal at best, the effort has served as a fine talking point for the college during fund raising campaigns—and student morale is enhanced enormously by the comparison.

Dr. Ernest Goldie's appointment to the Appleton faculty last September is illustrative of the importance that the college has attached to its business and economics program. A youngish man, who went directly from his doctoral studies to a teaching career at a modestly prominent Midwestern university, Dr. Goldie was enticed to come to Appleton by a substantial salary increase, the rank of associate professor, and glittering hopes for the future of the department and the college.

"Perhaps, Dr. Goldie, I might be able to track down the source—that is if you wouldn't mind my trying. After all, that's what a reference librarian is for."

"That's very kind of you, Mrs. Boyd. Very kind. It's a lot of work, but I do have other papers to correct, and if you don't mind taking it on, I'd be more than grateful to you."

"I'd love to help. It's quite possible I may be able to locate it in one of the periodical indexes."

"That's up to you, of course. I started by looking in the *Index of Economic Journals,* but gave it up for the direct approach." Dr. Goldie started for the door. "Let's hope I don't get any more papers like this one!"

"Oh, before you leave, Dr. Goldie, one question—why were you looking in the *American Economic Review*? I mean, is there some clue that made you check that particular periodical?"

"Well, the paper reads like an article—I'm convinced of that. And since I've already checked most of our books on Latin American economic development, I assumed that both *AER—American Economic Review*—and *Harvard Business Review* would be the next best places to check since I assign a fair amount of outside reading in both of them. Aside from that, the only other clue is the Treaty of Montevideo, which is mentioned in the paper. It's been in force since June, 1961—so I've been checking from that date."

"Wonderful, Dr. Goldie. That's a marvelous clue. I'll try to let you know by tomorrow afternoon what I've found."

Kay Boyd, possessor of a bachelor's degree in library science from a Canadian library school, has worked at Appleton College Library for the past three years. Approximately 50 years old, she spent several years working in the reference department of a large public library in Canada before her marriage to an American businessman, and it was not until the death of her husband three years ago that she returned to library work. When Mrs. Boyd came to Appleton, the reference department was in a state of atrophy. Since that time, she has worked hard to revitalize both student and faculty interest in the service, and while she has not had dramatic success, her enthusiasm and energy have impressed a reasonable number of people. Her staff consists of one full-time nonprofessional assistant, two part-time evening assistants, and Miss Kondazian, who looks after the Periodicals and Reserve Book Room.

Although Appleton College Library's reference collection can be honestly characterized as "mediocre," resources in the business and economics area are impressive for the size and caliber of the institution. This reflects the department chairman's insistence that research materials must be available to students and faculty if "departmental excellence" is to be maintained. In addition to the standard periodical indexes such as *Readers' Guide*, Public Affairs Information Service *Bulletin*, and *Social Science and Humanities Index*, the reference collection boasts *Business Periodicals Index, Cumulative Bibliography of Economic*

Books, Economic Abstracts, The Executive, F & S Index of Corporations and Industries, Index of Economic Journals, Index to Labor Union Periodicals, and the annual UNESCO series *International Bibliography of Economics.* Periodical holdings, too, reflect the business and economics department's desire to build a strong undergraduate program (*see* Appendix II).

After carefully reading the student's paper twice, Mrs. Boyd, happy to be useful to such an important member of the faculty as Dr. Goldie, agreed with the professor that indeed the paper was cribbed, that most likely it was copied from an article, and that the 1961 date was the only concrete clue offered by the text, although the phrase "after only a few years of operation" in the second paragraph was full of deep meaning. Lusting for the search, Mrs. Boyd approached the reference collection. "Let's see," she thought to herself, "both the *American Economic Review* and the *Harvard Business Review* are indexed in the *Readers' Guide,*" and she proceeded to check that index painstakingly from 1961 to the present under subject headings which she determined to be appropriate. She found several likely articles, but each turned out to be a false lead. Somewhat puzzled—perhaps annoyed is a more accurate description—she turned to *PAIS,* discovering that it too indexed both of the journals which Dr. Goldie had mentioned. However, again a careful check yielded no results.

The following day, when Mrs. Boyd found herself at the reference desk during a slack period, she decided to search the *International Bibliography of Economics.* In the course of her reference work, Mrs. Boyd rarely used any of the UNESCO annual bibliographies, finding them, she told students, "a bit confusing in arrangement." After spending considerable time with volumes of this bibliography, with no more success than she had had with the *Readers' Guide* or *PAIS,* Mrs. Boyd began to conclude that the offending student must have obtained the article—if, indeed, the student had used an article, a fact she was now beginning to doubt—from a private source. It did seem strange, since the nearest public library was small and inconsequential, and Appleton students had access to no other library in the immediate area, aside from the college library. However, a halfhearted investigation of *Business Periodicals Index* convinced Mrs. Boyd that she was up against a very, very clever criminal, to borrow Dr. Goldie's adjective. It was, therefore, with a great deal of reluctance that Mrs. Boyd telephoned Dr. Goldie that afternoon to report the negative results of her efforts.

■ After comparing the various bibliographic tools Mrs. Boyd searched
—and those which she neglected to search—consider whether or not she
approached the problem of locating the plagiarized source in the best
possible manner. How would you have handled this question? Is it possible to find the plagiarized source at Appleton College Library?

Appendix I

Page One of the Plagiarized Paper Submitted to Dr. Goldie

Under the traditional and now obsolete pattern of international trade, the
Latin American countries, as is still the case today, concentrated on commercial
dealings with the large industrial centers. Their economic contact with one
another was primarily limited to a small-scale interchange of certain primary
commodities, and industrialization in the region developed in watertight national
compartments. To serve the twofold aim of correcting the trend toward a
foreign-trade bottleneck and promoting the economic feasibility of the industrialization process, the establishment of a common market became imperative.

Concerted with notable speed, the Latin American Free Trade Association (LAFTA) after only a few years of operation has easily surpassed the minimum liberalization commitments stipulated in the Montevideo Treaty. But
owing to the sheer magnitude of the task the association is called upon to perform,
there is a real danger that its future rate of progress will become ponderous and
hedged about by caution. Such a rate might be acceptable if we could turn back
pages of history to those days in which the striking expansion of international
trade lent steady impetus to the Latin American economies. As matters stand at
present, however, when the serious obstacles of its development uncompromis-
ingly demand of Latin America a new outlook, firm determination, and boldly
constructive spirit, trade-liberalization progress has not achieved notable success.

It would be a mistake to question the intrinsic efficacy of the instruments established under the Montevideo Treaty. Important policy decisions are required, however, before this efficacy can be reflected in concrete achievements,
capable of counteracting the factors that can bring on early stagnation. The
present system of periodic selective negotiations may find the climate becoming
unpropitious, with the consequent risk that the entire endeavor may be reduced
to a series of narrow and halfhearted preferential arrangements.

This danger will persist until much clearer quantitative goals are established
for the reduction and elimination of tariffs and other restrictions within a specific
time limit. Failing that, the negotiations will be entirely lacking in the well-
defined terms of reference that are requisite to success. These targets should not
be set up in isolation, but must be accompanied by the groundwork for agree-

ments for complementary functioning, under which industries of great importance for development strategy could be programmed. Before proceeding with
these efforts, however, the concept of reciprocity must be clarified, and effective

Appendix II

Business and Economics Periodical Holdings at Appleton College Library

*Advanced Management/Office
  Executive* (1961–)
Advertising Age (unbound; retained
  5 years)
American Economic Review (1911–)
*American Journal of Economics and
  Sociology* (1941–)
American Statistician (1954–)
Banking (1962–)
Boston University Business Review
  (unbound; retained 5 years)
Business and Economics Review
  (1955–)
Business and Society (unbound;
  retained 3 years)
Business Management (1953–)
Business Quarterly (1939–)
Business Trends in New York State
  (unbound; retained 5 years)
Business Week (1947–)
Challenge (1954–)
Changing Times (1947–)
Commercial and Financial Chronicle
  (1962–)
Common Market (1961–)
Economic Intelligence (unbound;
  retained 3 years)
Economic Journal (1937–)
Economic World (1959–)
Economica (1921–)
Economist (1942–)
Federal Reserve Bulletin (1939–)
Financial Analysts Journal (1956–)
Forbes (1943–)
Fortune (1936–)
Harvard Business Review (1938–)
Harvard Business School Bulletin
  (1954–)

Indian Economic Journal (1961–)
Inter-American Economic Affairs
  (1963–)
International Commerce (1947–)
Journal of Business (1938–)
Journal of Business Education
  (1959–)
Journal of Common Market Studies
  (1965–)
Journal of Economic History (1945–)
Journal of Finance (1950–)
Journal of Marketing (1936–)
Journal of Property Management
  (1940–)
Journal of Political Economy (1935–)
*Journal of the American Statistical
  Association* (1954–)
Land Economics (1964–)
Management Quarterly (1961–)
Management Review (1914-26;
  1939–)
National Institute Economic Review
  (1960–)
Nation's Business (1942–)
New Englander (unbound; retained
  5 years)
Office Executive (1955–)
Oxford Economic Papers (1951–)
Personnel (1954–)
Personnel Administration (1952–)
Personnel Management (1954–)
Quarterly Journal of Economics
  (1939–)
*Quarterly Review of Economics and
  Business* (1961–)
Realtor (1960–)
Retail Control (1947–)
Review of Economic Studies (1954–)

Sales Management (1965–)

South African Journal of Economics (1940–)

Southern Economic Journal (1948–)

Soviet Studies (1963–)

Standard Bank Review (unbound; retained 3 years)

Survey of Current Business (unbound; retained until superceded by *Business Statistics*)

Wall Street Journal (1952-microfilm)

Yale Economic Essays (1960–)

8

The Population Explosion

For years, the Trapelo Free Public Library had been little more than a gloomy eyesore on Stillman Street—a dirty gray, barn-like building which supplied comforting light fiction and best sellers to ladies craving vicarious romance and escape. And, too, the building served as a place for students from nearby Trapelo High to meet and, occasionally, do their homework. For the great majority of Trapelo's 26,500 residents, however, the library was akin to a haunted house, somber and usually deserted, presided over by elderly ghosts who traveled under the label "librarians."

This despairing picture began to change six or seven months ago when Raymond DeSales, an energetic young man with ideas and a brand new library degree, arrived on the scene as city librarian. Two years ago a man with DeSales' qualifications and ambitions would not have chosen to come to Trapelo—and Trapelo (pronounced Tra-PELL-o) would not have asked him. But two years can change the personality of a community, and Trapelo, once one of the most politically unwholesome cities in Pennsylvania, was currently in the midst of civic improvement and political reform. The now infamous School Board Scandal which indeed did take on upper-case magnitude, involving a majority of the board's members in a lucrative textbook purchasing kickback operation, seemed to be the final outrage, the final cavalier misuse of the public trust which the citizens of Trapelo would tolerate. A relatively minor incident, the Scandal touched off a spirit of change in the community. A grassroots reform group calling itself the Citizens Party, composed of people of every stripe—political amateurs, self-appointed do-gooders, worried housewives, believers in the democratic remedy—who wished to demonstrate their faith in the principle that

40

you can fight city hall, finally wrested control of the municipal governmental machinery from the local Boss Tweed and his cronies. A city manager was hired to run the city with non-partisan efficiency; a new school board was elected and began the arduous job of improving an inadequate educational system; a new chief of police was appointed to replace Chief Iffley, who had found it expedient to close his eyes to honest graft. In a word, Trapelo was on the move. And, although the shanties and broken-down houses in "Little Poland" remained, although unemployment still stood at a rigid seven percent, and although welfare rolls remained swollen (see Appendix I), the good citizens of Trapelo believed that the initial steps had been taken to transform a lackluster coal city into a good, decent place in which to live.

While the seven member library board continued intact after the reformers came to power, pressure for improvement of the library's services and facilities was exerted by the new school board. Jonathan Kennebee, longtime chairman of the library board of trustees, was a practical man, sensitive to the vagaries of public opinion. He saw quite clearly that the "new boys" would have a new kind of public library—with or without Jonathan Kennebee. So, he accommodated himself to the spirit of reform. Accommodation to reform, however, did not come as easily to the Misses Overlook and Motte, two spinsters who had shared the duties of librarian for an unremembered number of years. For several months, the situation was an unhappy one for the ladies and the library board, but the problem resolved itself nicely when the team of Overlook and Motte announced their joint retirement, in order to end, they said, the board's "unjustified interference with their work." After considerable fumbling, the board eventually advertised for a qualified librarian and finally hired young Raymond DeSales.

DeSales, in the course of his interview with the library board, promised to turn the library "inside out, making it a force for education and recreation in the community," while warning that, "the job can't be done overnight—books, gentlemen, don't just fly onto the shelves, and it'll take sometime before the public realizes that the library can serve its intellectual and leisure needs." In addition, he noted that current library expenditures were hopelessly below professional minimum requirements. DeSales suggested that working to rectify this situation should be the board's first order of business after hiring a librarian.

Within six months of his arrival in Trapelo, DeSales had moved on a number of fronts to make the library "a force for education and recreation." The dirty gray building on Stillman Street was painted a taste-fully rich red—"to make people notice it," the new library director told his board. A professional children's librarian was hired, the board, at DeSales' urging, securing an emergency appropriation from the city manager's office. A weekly library news column, written by DeSales, be-gan to appear in the *Trapelo Trumpet*. A Sunday afternoon radio show called "Books are My Beat" featured DeSales talking about new titles available in the library. The book and periodical collection was slowly being improved by DeSales' careful attention to book selection. The existing collection was in the process of being checked against standard lists as a guide for retrospective purchasing (at the present time, DeSales is checking the National Council of Teachers of English's *College and Adult Reading List* against his holdings), and, concurrently, the collection was being weeded. Perhaps DeSales' most dramatic move, however, was to conduct a drive for increased library registration—a campaign which resulted in nearly 6,000 newly registered borrowers. And, only last week, the library initiated a summer reading program for young people.

Recently, when reporting to the library board on the progress of his various projects to improve library service, DeSales pointed out that, "Our book collection now contains almost 15,000 titles—or 1,500 more than when I took over. This means that almost 80 percent of our book fund is exhausted for this year. Next year, we'll need a budgetary in-crease of one hundred percent. And, because I'm forced to spend a great amount of time processing books which could be better used in more productive ways—like getting on with selecting a Polish collection —I suggest that we should plan to add a cataloger to the staff next year." DeSales went on to explain that circulation had doubled during his six months at the library and "the registration campaign brought the total number of registered users to over 7,500, or 28.3 percent of the people in the city. I try to give one hour a day to reference service for the kids in the evening, but soon we'll need a reference librarian, too." The board promised to see what could be done about increasing the library's budget for the following year.

After this particular meeting had concluded, Chairman Kennebee told DeSales that the library board was "very, very pleased with the way you're building up the library, Ray. We're going to fight for the money you need, and we'll damn well get it. A lot of people that I never thought would set foot inside the library have told me how nice the library's coming along. The only complaint I've heard is about some of the books you're buying. That 'Naked' thing, for example."

"Well, Mr. Kennebee, *Naked Lunch* may be offensive to some people, but it's an important book—something of a modern classic now— and if we're to have a good library we can't have any censorship. That's exactly why I asked the board to subscribe to the ALA Bill of Rights at our first meeting."

"I wholeheartedly support that statement, Ray, but if we're to get you the money for all those things you mentioned tonight, then we can't go around offending people. Miss Zimmerman mentioned the other day that that Naked Lunch book shouldn't be in the library. Said it's dirty. And you know that her brother's close to the city manager."

"Don't worry, Mr. Kennebee. I intend to get to writing that book selection policy one of these days that'll cover us if this kind of criticism gets out of hand." (*See* Appendix II.)

The day was sunny and warm. Raymond DeSales found it difficult to concentrate on reading book reviews. Besides, he had little money left to buy books for the remainder of the year. "At least the place is beginning to look like a library." He broke off his musing, opening the window of his office as high as possible.

"Mr. DeSales?"

DeSales turned and faced a man and a woman whom he had never seen before standing in the doorway of his office. "Yes? What can I do for you?" He tried to remember if he had any appointments.

"Mr. DeSales, I'm Bob Earborn. And this is Mrs. Fox. We're from TRAGIC. A young lady downstairs told us we could find you up here. We found your door open and, well, we're here."

"TRAGIC? Oh, won't you sit down. Just let me get another chair."

EARBORN: "The Trapelo Action Group for Inspiring Contraception. You may have heard our advertisements on the local radio station."

DESALES: "It doesn't ring a bell—but then I've only been in Trapelo for a short time. I'm really just getting to know the community."

EARBORN: "Briefly, Mr. DeSales, TRAGIC is a private, nonprofit organization established eighteen months ago which is concerned with the high birthrate not only in Trapelo—although this is where our efforts are concentrated—but the United States and the world. We feel that if we meet this problem locally—and other communities follow our lead—we can avoid the possibility of federal interference, which will undoubtedly come if someone doesn't act. And the high cost of bureaucracy is something we can all do without, I guess."

DESALES: "That's interesting, because I just ordered a few books for the library on that subject not long ago. You're probably familiar with Bromley's *Catholics and Birth Control* and Dr. Rock's book."

MRS. FOX: "Oh yes—we have lists of all the books like that. The trouble is the information changes so quickly. I mean Rock is terribly dated, don't you think?"

EARBORN: "TRAGIC, Mr. DeSales, publishes a good deal of literature in pamphlet form for local distribution and, naturally, we're concerned about getting our up-to-date information to as wide an audience as possible. With welfare costs running skyhigh here in Trapelo due to illegitimacy and unemployment, it's really important—imperative —we reach low income groups. And, since we've heard that you're really doing great things with the library, we—TRAGIC—hoped you may agree to add our publications to the library. At no expense to the library, of course."

DESALES: "Why I'd be delighted to have them. At the moment, I'm in the process of building up the vertical file, and I can use any pamphlet type material you have. I really couldn't promise to catalog any of your publications—at the present time, it's just too expensive in terms of time."

MRS. FOX: "What is this 'vertical file'? A display rack?"

DESALES: "No, it's a metal filing cabinet where I keep ephemeral material—under broad subjects. Like birth control, for example."

EARBORN: "It's very kind of you, Mr. DeSales, to agree to take our publications, but wouldn't it be even better to put them out where people can see them, such as you do with the new books. We noticed your attractive display as we entered the building. I know something about marketing technique, Mr. DeSales, and I can assure you that nothing beats displaying the product. And libraries can do so much along this line. As I'm sure you're aware—and I don't mean to be critical of your predecessors—this library has dragged its heels as a real source for information. Now, thanks to you, we're finally getting a twentieth-century library."

DESALES: "Well—that's very kind of you to say. We're trying. But

I don't think I can present material which, ah, may not be acceptable to certain religious groups."

MRS. FOX: "Oh, that's no real problem any longer. With the new types of birth control pills, drugs, and devices available—all described in our literature—birth control is virtually acceptable to all major faiths, those bound by the Pope's encyclical to the contrary, of course."

DESALES: "New devices?" DeSales blushed slightly.

MRS. FOX: "Ah ha! Mr. DeSales, I caught you! You're *not* up-to-date on this matter. Devices the size of threads or microscopic dots containing antifertility hormones are available. They can be surgically placed in the female's arm or leg. In fact, recent clinical research shows that these hormones can be injected by needles. As far as the pill is concerned—"

EARBORN: "Excuse me, Mrs. Fox, but I think we should tell Mr. DeSales that our information is highly reliable and up-to-date. The devices which Mrs. Fox mentioned are made of plastic or wax and being porous they constantly release tiny amounts of the antifertility hormone into the bloodstream. Let me show you our literature. We have three pamphlets and a select bibliography." Earborn gave DeSales a copy of each of the pamphlets and the bibliography. The publications were attractively printed and, as far as DeSales was concerned, appeared to be formidably scientific. The three page bibliography, he observed, contained several books which he had purchased for the library.

MRS. FOX: "And, of course, anyone morally opposed to birth control or who agree with the Pope would simply pass up our literature."

DESALES: "The library *is* an educational institution, and even though it's a somewhat delicate issue, libraries can't go around with their heads in the sand." He became resolute. "I'll be happy to give our cooperation to TRAGIC. In fact, I read just the other day that some scientists studying population said that we'll soon be in a new dark age if we don't control the population explosion."

MRS. FOX: "I saw that, too. The world's population in 1960 was almost three billion. By 1980 it will be over *four* billion—and by 2000, over *six* billion. That's based on United Nations figures we cite in our literature."

DESALES: "And the article I read said that if we don't do something, man may be driven to *cannibalism*."

EARBORN: "I can't tell you how pleased we are—TRAGIC is—that you'll cooperate, Mr. DeSales. It's very public spirited of you. I'll have our literature—for free distribution—sent over in the morning. Did we settle on a place to display it?"

DESALES: "What I'd like to do is organize a display, using your material and some of the books I've bought, and maybe some articles from *Life* and *Look* and so on, for the adult reading room. How's that? And, after the display's over, I'll simply put your literature on the free table—where we put things that patrons can take free of charge."

EARBORN: "That will do very nicely, Mr. DeSales. Very nicely. And you will be sure to indicate by sign that our literature can be taken gratis?"

DESALES: "Sure. That'll be the purpose, as I see it, of the display. Usually library displays are just innocuous. This one will have a real social purpose."

Approximately ten days after the birth control display had been placed in the adult reading room, two letters appeared in the *Trapelo Trumpet* decrying the action.

To the Editor:

I want to register a strong public protest about the library on Stillman Street. Yesterday, my daughter sneaked a booklet home which describes, in vivid detail, how to go about birth control. After I found it, she admitted getting it at the library after school. I checked for myself as I could not believe it, and found that several different booklets are openly available for our teeners to pick up and read. The librarians do not even know who is taking what. I am not the only Mother who is concerned about these booklets. There has been a lot of noise lately about our FREE library. I think it is nothing but an agent of filth when decent people and their teeners cannot visit the library without being bombarded with disgusting sex booklets. Something should be done!

CONCERNED MOTHER

To the Editor:

On my most recent visit to the Trapelo Free Public Library on Stillman Street, I was confronted with a display of literature which insinuates people should practice birth control. And what is more, it tells them how to go about it, with all the murderous methods described in exacting, scientific detail. These materials are free for the taking. If our young people, and older ones for that matter, are to go to School and Church to learn the moral precepts of our Saviour, and then learn at the Library that human life is not sacred, not the Greatest Gift, it is up to responsible adults to protect their innocence in a sometimes unkind world. The *Bible*, which is not on display at our Library, says: "Be not deceived, God is not mocked: For whatsoever a Man soweth, that shall he also reap." (Epistle of Paul to the Galatians).

V. PAUL EMSELLA
Sunday School Teacher

■ The following morning, Raymond DeSales received a telephone call from Jonathan Kennebee. Kennebee's tone was shrill, his voice angry and quarrelsome.

How can DeSales defend his treatment of TRAGIC's literature? Consider DeSales' argument and conviction that the public library is an educational institution. Specifically, what are the library's responsibilities and limitations when dealing with socially controversial materials? Evaluate the veracity of TRAGIC's literature based on the information which Earborn and Mrs. Fox gave to DeSales during their conversation. Investigate Pennsylvania law regarding distribution of birth control information. Finally, since DeSales has not yet composed a written book selection policy for the Trapelo Free Public Library, write one for him (*see* Appendix II).

Appendix I

Selected Statistics—Trapelo

Racial data (US Census)		Religious data (local statistics)	
White	24,973	Protestant	14,921
Negro	1,509	Roman Catholic	10.486
Other	18	Jewish	434
Foreign Stock	9,759	Other	1,131
Foreign Born	5,011		

Occupational data (US Census)		*Welfare data* (local statistics)	
Professional, etc.	502	14% of all families in Trapelo received	
Managerial	431	welfare last year.	
Clerical, etc.	1,103	Local	9 %
Sales	601	Public	7.4
Foremen	1,120	Private	5
Laborers	3,747	State	9
Service	582	Federal	12.5

Births and Deaths

(US Census)

During the last decade, the population of Trapelo increased by 4,391. There was an excess of births over deaths of 8,417. During the same period, there was a net out-migration of 4,026.

Appendix II

Book Selection Policy

"Every library should have a written statement of policy, covering the selection and maintenance of its collection of books and of nonbook materials." So states the ALA *Public Library Service* (1956). Compose a book selection policy statement for the Trapelo Free Public Library, noting such aspects of policy as: objectives of book selection; evaluative criteria used to select; procedures; treatment of controversial material; responsibility and final authority for selection; gift materials; withdrawals; special collections and departments.

9

Dirty Books

Raymond DeSales was irritated and nervous as he sat in his office reading the *Trumpet's* editorial.

Since the unfortunate episode with TRAGIC and its birth control literature nearly a year ago, DeSales' plans for remaking the Trapelo Free Public Library had not proceeded as smoothly as he would have liked. Some progress, true, had been made in several areas. A part-time cataloger had been hired, relieving DeSales of that "onerous chore," as he put it. Circulation figures continued to rise—not perhaps as dramatically as they had during DeSales' initial months as librarian when enthusiasm for the new director's restless campaign to make a better library was at its peak; nevertheless, he was usually able to report modest monthly increases in the number of books loaned, much to the pleasure of his library board. Funds had been appropriated, after acerbic debate by the board, to convert the old newspaper and periodical room into a comfortably furnished browsing room. Recently opened, the new browsing room houses the library's avant-garde fiction, art books, and recent issues of popular and arty magazines. Although pleased with the browsing room and its collection, DeSales considered the whole venture as only a partial victory for progress, since the board had forced him to abandon his idea of permitting smoking in that area of the library.

There were other setbacks, too. DeSales' disappointment was severe when the library board rejected his proposal to hire a professional reference librarian. "How can we make the community aware of the potential of the library as an information center if we're only giving an hour or so a day to reference service?" The board was sorry, but funds were not available at the present time for another professional position at the library. After all, the board held, library salaries had increased in Trapelo by almost 300 percent since DeSales' appointment a year and a half ago. The book fund, too, had not risen fast enough to suit DeSales, who complained to the board that his retrospective buying projects, necessary if the library was to even begin to meet its steadily increasing obligations to the city's public school students, were languishing for lack of funds. Jonathan Kennebee, chairman of the library board, explained that the board's hands were tied—that DeSales would have to do his level best with the money he already had at his disposal.

And now there was this editorial. DeSales lit a cigarette and reread it, occasionally making a notation in the margin of the paper.

DIRTY BOOKS

It may not be in vogue these days to call a dirty book "dirty." But let's face it, some books are dirty, full of disgusting language and descriptions best left in the gutter where they came from. Nothing in this world, no verbal trick or moral sleight of hand, will make them "clean." Experts talk about redeeming social "importance" and community "standards," jargon introduced by the Supreme Court of the United States, no less, but this kind of sputtering is nothing more than a red herring, beclouding the real issue. Dirty books serve no good purpose for society and its members, beyond enriching those who publish and peddle such slime. Dirty books can—and do— cause terrible harm to the moral fabric of society. Individuals, *especially young people*, are encouraged to try out the violent, immoral, and perverted acts they read about. The *Trumpet* daily hears of criminal and immoral behavior which is directly inspired by ideas and representations found in dirty and sadistic books and magazines. Obviously, even the Supreme Court finally woke up to this fact when it condemned the well-known pornographer Ginzburg to prison sometime ago.

✼ ✼ ✼ ✼ ✼ ✼

It may surprise some of Trapelo's decent citizens to learn that the Free Public Library is spending hundreds of dollars of tax monies on dirty books this year. The so-called "browsing" room which opened last month is little more than a collection of choice erotica, thinly veiled as "contemporary literature" and "modern art." Decent people anywhere—and we hope that includes Trapelo—do not want to read such sick perversion as *City of Night, The Ticket That Exploded,* or *The Story of O,* to name but a few of the most offensive books in that room. It is not enough to claim, as the librarian naively does, that the books in that room are limited to adults, when any teenager 16 or over can obtain an adult library card to use the *adult* library. Lewd and salacious books of this nature will find their way to our young people in limited numbers—such is the power of the pornography industry. But by placing these books *on the open shelves* of the library, a venerable institution becomes venereal—a vendor of that which is harmful and prurient. In addition, by so doing the library flies in the face of the celebrated Ginzburg ruling by the Supreme Court and the more recent Ginsberg case. Trapelo has proved that it can clean up City Hall. Now the *Trumpet* calls upon the librarian and the Board of Trustees to take appropriate steps to clean up the Free Public Library. Or the citizenry will have to take on that task, too.

DeSales lit another cigarette. He had realized that the browsing room collection would cause some criticism, although he had felt confident that his book selection policy, formulated soon after the TRAGIC affair, would serve to protect the library from any wholesale criticism. A liberal document which stressed both the importance of the freedom to read and the inherent dangers of censorship in any form, DeSales' book selection policy had been endorsed by the library board after considerable discussion. Armed with this statement of policy and the ALA Bill of Rights, DeSales had been able to effectively handle isolated attempts to have this or that book removed from the library. In one instance, he was successful in convincing an irate mother that the *ABZ of Love* should be in the library's collection, even though she disapproved it for her son. In a similar manner, he had saved the *Evergreen Review* from the would-be censor.

But now this. The editorial was a call to insurrection. Its hysterical tone was all the more surprising to DeSales since he had a passing acquaintanceship with Bob Perry, the *Trumpet's* editor, and had once briefly discussed censorship with him and had been pleased to discover that Perry opposed, with some hazy qualifications, restrictions on the availability of books and other materials to the public. Now this. "Better get in touch with Kennebee before he gets his nose out of joint." DeSales knew that backing from the board may collapse if public opinion took up the

Trumpet's peroration—he was well aware that he was still an outsider while each member of the board was, first and last, a Trapelian.

DeSales dialed Kennebee's office, hoping, in spite of himself, that the old man would not be in.

"Kennebee and Sparkill, contractors. Good afternoon."

"Hello, Miss Marshall. This is Ray DeSales at the public library. Could I speak to Mr. Kennebee?"

"Just a min, Mr. DeSales."

DeSales chewed his thumb and wondered how in the world he ever got into librarianship. He remembered: he liked people and books.

"Hello, Ray." Kennebee's voice thundered into the phone. "Now before you say a thing, I've seen it. And you damn well better get rid of those three books and any others like them—fast!"

"Now wait *a* minute, Mr. Kennebee. It's—I—this is the time to be firm—to close ranks. To just—"

"*You* wait a minute, Ray." Kennebee's voice softened a bit. "Look, son, I'm going to put it to you straight. I haven't worked in the business world all my life without learning that you got to bend—compromise— sometimes. I warned you a good long time ago that those damn books you were getting in there would blow up." Kennebee stopped for a gulp of air.

"I appreciate what you're saying, sir, but to give in to this kind of emotionalism would only undo all the good work we've done over the past eighteen months. As I see it, we've—"

"Ray. Listen. I've talked to two-three other board people—Stultz and Winn for two—and they don't want any part of those books. You remember what happened with those sex pamphlets you had in there? Now I—"

"They were *not* 'sex' pamphlets, Mr. Kennebee, and you know that. But forget that for a minute. Just hear me out, will you please. I've always believed, and I thought the board agreed, that books can't hurt people, kids included. Perry's editorial—or whoever wrote it—is full of out-and-out misstatements of fact. It's ridiculous! And I intend to answer that editorial point-by-point."

"I know how you feel, Ray. I don't like this censorship business anymore than you do. I like Robert Perry even less. But less than that I— let's just say I like smut even less. Why if I so much as caught my grandchildren with that 'Naked' thing or those other books, I'd tan the livin' tar out of them."

"That's your privilege, sir, but I still intend to answer that editorial point-by-point. I intend to show up that piece of hysteria for what it really is."

"Answer any damn thing you want, Ray—just get those books out of the library. Take them home and read them yourself!"

■ How would you analyze the position DeSales has taken vis-a-vis the *Trumpet's* editorial? Kennebee? Is it possible for DeSales to refute the editorial's main contentions? Pay particular attention to the assertion that "Dirty books can—and do—cause terrible harm to the moral fabric of society." What scientific evidence exists on both sides of this question? Why have social scientists been unsuccessful, thus far, in reaching definite conclusions about the causal effects of obscenity?

10

International Poker

"I'm sorry to bother you, Mrs. Baker, but this is something of an emergency. Dr. Moseley just called from his home, and he needs the contents of a particular document rather quickly." Edward Nixon, a graduate teaching assistant in the history department at Green University, outlined the crisis situation. "He's writing an article on the diplomatic maneuvering which preceded the Franco-Prussian War, and there's a note or letter that Francis Joseph of Austria-Hungary sent to Napoleon III in 1869, which he wants to check. It's a reply to a letter from Napoleon."

Janice Baker, librarian in charge of the History Library at Green, knew Nixon as a serious, conscientious young man whom Dr. Moseley occasionally used to do his legwork. Mrs. Baker shifted the telephone receiver as she searched for a note pad. "Where are you?"

"Where am I? I'm here—at the history department. Dr. Mosely called here to ask me to check some books in his office—he thought I might be able to find a copy of the note, but when I couldn't he suggested I call you."

"I see. Now about this note. What did you say the date was? 1869?"

"According to Dr. Mosely, the exact date of the Napoleon letter to Francis Joseph was September 24th, 1869. Of course, he doesn't know exactly when Francis Joseph sent his reply, but obviously it must have been before the end of the year."

"And he wants the text of Francis Joseph's reply?"

"That's right."

"Now what kind of note was this? There was probably a great deal of correspondence between them at that time. Was it a note about the coming war or what?"

"According to Dr. Moseley, the letter from Napoleon to Francis Joseph said that he, Napoleon, would aid the Austro-Hungarians if they were attacked by another power, and that he wouldn't make any international agreements without first consulting them. See, Napoleon realized that France was becoming increasingly isolated, and he was trying to build some kind of alliance against Prussia and Russia. Except, in the end, Bismarck was a better poker player."

"He has the text of that letter—Napoleon's to Francis Joseph. Is that right?"

"Yes, that's right. Francis Joseph's reply to Napoleon's letter, Dr. Moseley thinks, was noncommittal and evasive, but of course he has to see the contents to be absolutely sure."

"And Dr. Moseley needs this right away?"

"Yes, as soon as possible. I told him that one of us would call him as soon as we located the document. By the way, he said not to bother looking in Snyder's *Documents*—he's already checked it at home."

"Just one more question before you hang up. How important is this correspondence? I mean, is it significant historically?"

"Is it significant historically? I really can't answer that. To *me* it isn't, but maybe it is to Dr. Moseley."

The History Library, one of a number of separately housed departmental and divisional collections at Green which complement the university's 1,500,000 volume main library, is devoted primarily to specialized research materials in the field. Due more to tradition rather than formal policy, the collection has emphasized European historiography over other areas. For example, the library includes a complete set of *Almanach de Gotha, Revue Historique* since 1911, most volumes of *Jahresberichte der Geschichtswissenschaft,* and all annual issues of *Jahresberichte für deutsche Geschichte.* Mrs. Baker, a trained librarian, has been working in the History Library since her husband became a doctoral student at Green nearly two years ago. Although she has no background in history beyond a few courses on the undergraduate level, her adequate knowledge of French, German, and Spanish secured her the position.

■ What sources should Mrs. Baker search for the Francis Joseph-Napoleon III diplomatic exchange? Particularly, what sources of original documents should be checked? Are there any sources of German historical documents which may be helpful, aside from Louis Snyder's *Documents of German History?* Any for French documents? Is there a collection of official documents of the Austro-Hungarian Empire? Allowing that Mrs. Baker will have available the major published collections of original documents for the countries involved, will she be able to locate the Francis Joseph communication? Investigate the problems which confront historians and librarians when dealing with original documents—especially official government documents.

11

Nothing But The Best

Roy Hosmer, a tall, balding man in his early fifties, entered the brightly lighted East Branch of the Varnum Public Library. After a slight hesitation, he approached a young girl seated behind the circulation desk.

"Excuse me, Miss."

The young girl looked up from the book she was reading. "Good evening. Can I help you?"

"Yes, thanks. I'd like to see the books about colleges. Could you show me where they're kept?"

"Ones that tell about fees and that sort of thing?"

"Yes, that's the kind of books I had in mind."

The girl, a part-time evening library assistant, quickly led the inquirer to the reference collection and pointed to a specific section. "These reference books—the ones numbered 378—are about colleges and universities. A lot of the high school students use this one." She handed Hosmer the latest edition of *Lovejoy's College Guide*. "Excuse me, now. I have to get back to the circulation desk—my helper's still shelving books."

"Thanks very much, Miss. I think this'll be just what I'm looking for." However, when the branch library closed for the evening an hour later, Hosmer had not succeeded in locating the information he wanted.

Varnum, an industrial city located in one of the Midwestern states, is a trade center for nearly 80,000 people who live in the city and surrounding area. The current census report indicates that 51,281 persons live within the city boundary, a seven percent increase over the previous figure. While only approximately ten percent (or less than 2,000 persons,) of Varnum's labor force is classified as professional, almost 45 percent of the city's high school students seek some form of higher education, many attending the local state college.

About a week after Roy Hosmer's visit to the East Branch, Miss Julia Locke, Varnum's library director, received the following letter.

20 Dore Street
Varnum
April 3, 19—

Dear Miss Locke:

You do not know me, but I believe that you do know Mr. Joseph Rockingham of Lorna Handbag Company? I am a foreman at Lorna and Mr. Rockingham told me you might be able to help me find out some information about colleges for Sarah my daughter, since he knows you from the Service Club. I was in my own library the other night but could not find anything. My wife, who passed away two years ago next month, always wanted our Sarah to go to the best college she could, but the guidance counselor at the High School says Sarah should go to Varnum. Now I know there must be better colleges for Sarah to go to and Mr. Rockingham said you could give me a list of the ten best girls colleges in the country. Sarah is a good girl and she has always done very good on her tests at the High School. Her Mother always wanted Sarah to get the best education possible second to none at a girls college so she could study better without the boys always around.

I am sorry to bother you this way about my problem but it is important to me that Sarah goes to a college that is the best in our fine country. Thanking you for your kind attention.

Sincerely yours,
Roy M. Hosmer

Miss Locke sent Hosmer's letter to Brian Olcott, director of information services for the Varnum system, with the following note attached.

To: Mr. Olcott
From: Julia A. Locke

Brian, would you take care of this inquiry. Write Mr. Hosmer a nice, helpful letter. Will *Barron's Profiles* help?

JAL

Varnum Public Library, with financial support slightly below American Library Association recommendations for achieving minimum standards, has been capably administered during the past eleven years by Miss

Locke. Although a new central library building is urgently needed, two new branches have been constructed over the past five years—the East Branch with a 25,000 volume capacity being the more recent of the two. In addition, the system maintains one other branch library. In all three branches, the emphasis is on popular and recreational reading material rather than serious, scholarly nonfiction. Moreover, both Miss Locke and Brian Olcott believe that the central library should be the bibliographic and reference center for the community, and, consequently, branch library reference collections are limited to no more than ninety or a hundred indispensable fact-finding tools and standard trade bibliographies.

Because the Varnum High School Library purchases very selectively among the available reference publications due to budgetary limitations, the public library receives heavy student use, and it is for this reason that the central library buys such materials as the important college and university directories and guides. The educational guides, it should be pointed out, are frequently consulted by parents and students to aid in the selection of prospective colleges or universities, a procedure that in many instances is necessary because the city's high school employs only two qualified guidance counselors for almost 4,000 students.

■ In addition to writing a letter answering Mr. Hosmer's inquiry, this case involves a comparative analysis of the major American educational guides and other materials which may be used when approaching this problem. Aside from these considerations, other aspects of the case require comment. Should a branch library as large as East have the resources—both human and bibliographic—to deal with questions such as Hosmer's? What is the public library's responsibility to Hosmer and his daughter? Should public libraries have written policies governing the librarian's role as adviser or counselor?

12

Physical, Biological, Or Behavioral?

"—and so, you see, quite apart from desiring to understand the concepts involved in system analysis, I would be reprehensive if I neglected securing the articles, reading them, and, of course, communicating my personal comments to Professor Russell. You see, I met him this past summer while holidaying on the Isle of Man and we became rather fast friends, actually. In point of fact, this is my *second* letter from him since my return to Osceola. You see, Man has multitudinous artifacts—crosses, stone monuments, and the like—which date from the Neolithic period, and to listen to him propounding his theories about system analysis among those ancient relics was an exquisite experience. A perfect blending of the modern scholar seeking Truth amid the ineluctable Past. Actually—"

"That's all very interesting, but what was that author again? Now where's my—got it—all right now, the author was—?" Jacqueline Brinton reference librarian at the Osceola College Library, waited, resembling a stenographer waiting for dictation.

"Thompson. T-h-o-m-p-s-o-n." The young man, a student at Osceola whom Miss Brinton remembered from the previous school year, crisply enunciated each letter, and officiously watched to see that she copied the name correctly.

"And you say that your professor friend mentioned no specific titles? No specific periodicals?"

Passing her a letter, the student permitted himself a wry smile. "As you can see—here—he has only casually jotted down the reference, assuming that—incorrectly, I must confess to my chagrin—that I have some rather expert knowledge of such literature. Scholars, you know, rather assume with authors ever lightly on their tongues that their fellows will understand. It forever makes me—"

"His handwriting is barely legible. What's this word?"

The student bent over for a close look. Miss Brinton noticed that he had bad breath. "Similarities. It says, 'Suggest you investigate Thompson's articles on *similarities* between the human transition from adolescence to adulthood and the climatic transition from winter to summer.' Then he goes on to make a funny about us Americans calling autumn, "fall." He does have a jolly bad hand, eh? My experience has been that all Englishmen are rather cryptic of hand, actually."

"And this similarity between age in people and the changes of the seasons is called 'systems analysis'?"

"System. No 's' on it. Yes, apparently that is an example. As Professor Russell explained it to me—among the relics on Man, you know—the idea involves discovery of interrelationships, or common principles, among environmental conditions—natural phenomena, actually—and human behavior."

"Like comparing the growth and development of trees to man?"

"Jolly good! That's it exactly. You see, Professor Russell says—"

"I have someone else waiting. I'll see what I can do about locating these Thompson articles. Let me have your name and dorm number and I'll notify you when I've located them."

"I shall be frightfully grateful."

"It may take sometime—this Thompson may be British, since your professor friend is. You may, if I can't locate them, simply have to write to him and get the citations."

"I would much—much, much—prefer not to have to do that. You see, quite apart from being rude—he *may* feel I were criticizing him—I am quite eager to begin a serious investigation of system analysis, and it may be sometime until Professor Russell will get around to answering my missive. He *is* a rather busy man, you know, actually."

In its early days (1837-1896), Osceola, like many southern educational institutions of the period, was both a college and a preparatory school. Today, Osceola College enrolls upwards of a thousand male students, offering the bachelor of arts degree to sons of well-to-do families, from both the North and South, who are concerned that the attitudes and graces of the Southern Gentleman be preserved. High tuition rates and a healthy endowment fund allow the college to support an eminently qualified faculty of over one hundred—two-thirds of whom hold the doctoral degree, which, according to Osceola's bulletin, is twice the national average.

The college library, named for the late George F. Stedman, a trustee of the school from 1894 to 1959, is a modern, air-conditioned building which houses a book collection of 155,000, over 600 currently received serials, and a wide selection of American and foreign newspapers. In addition, the library maintains several special collections, the most prominent being the Ada Percy Worthington manuscript collection, which contains some 300 items of incunabula.

The reference collection, carefully selected and maintained by Miss Brinton, is designed to meet the immediate reference requirements of Osceola's students and faculty. However, when engaged in research projects, faculty members at Osceola more often than not make arrangements to use the Jeffers University Library, (approximately one million volumes), which is located some thirty miles from Osceola.

It was not until the following morning that Jacqueline Brinton was able to begin searching for references to articles by a Thompson which presumably illustrated a comparison between man and climate. She spent two tedious, frustrating hours on the question, and then gave up. That afternoon, she mentioned the problem to one of her reference assistants, Sarah Harmony.

"The big problem, Sarah, is that I don't really know what I'm looking for. System analysis exists, because I found headings in *Social Science and Humanities Index* and elsewhere for it—but I can't pinpoint exactly what the best index is to check. I looked in the catalog and we have only one book—something called *The New Utopians* by a Robert Boguslaw. It has footnotes, but no Thompson showed up. I checked *Books in Print* but no Thompson on system analysis. Same with *British Books in Print*. I know you like interesting questions, so if you want to work on it for awhile, go ahead. But don't spend an inordinate amount of time on it —the boy's a priggish little know-it-all and it'll serve him right if we can't find it. Besides, he can always write to his professor friend and get the citations."

Miss Harmony indicated that the question did interest her, and that she would spend a little time on it that afternoon if things were fairly quiet at the reference desk.

■ If you were Miss Harmony, how would you proceed to locate citations to the Thompson articles on system analysis, keeping in mind the general character of Osceola's library? Outline your procedure, step-by-step. Criticize Miss Brinton's approach to the problem.

13

Offensive References

"Excuse me, young woman. Are you on duty here? Young woman!"

Alice Lothrop, reference assistant at the South Market Branch of the Orehard Public Library, was helping a high school student find biographical information about Robert Frost when a grating, high-pitched voice interrupted her. She turned and greeted a wrinkled, little woman of perhaps seventy or seventy-five, the owner of the squeaky voice. "Yes? I'm the reference librarian on duty. Can I help you or—"

"Yes you certainly can, young woman. Have you examined the books in this room? Do you know that you have books in this room that could start a race riot?"

"I'm afraid I don't understand—these are *reference* books, and I'm sure that—"

"Don't pussyfoot with me, young woman. Who's in charge of these books? Who's responsible for the books in this library? Answer me that." The old lady cocked her head, waiting to hear Miss Lothrop's reply.

"Well, madam, we have a committee that selects all the books for the whole Orehard system—but I'm afraid I still don't understand what—"

"Have you and this *committee* ever looked closely at this book?" She pointed to *A New Dictionary of Quotations on Historical Principles from Ancient and Modern Sources,* selected and edited by H. L. Mencken and published by Knopf in 1942. It was lying open on one of the study tables.

"Of course I know that book. What's wrong with it? It's just a quotation dictionary, similar to many others we have."

"Have you, young woman, ever looked closely at some of these *quotations?*"

"Well, I usually use *Bartlett's,* but—"

"Let me show you *exactly* what I'm referring to. See this—and this!" Under the subject "Negro" on pages 843-45, there appeared a number of quotations from various sources which contained the word "nigger."

"I must admit I've never come across this section of quotations before."

"You people in the library ought to look more closely at what you go putting in our library. James—my grandson—came home the other day from school reciting some of these—some of this *poetry*. He confessed that he and some of his friends were down here looking through this book. Devilish—that's what these youngsters of today are. Always looking for trouble. James's school has many colored students and this sort of book in the wrong hands could cause a *great* deal of trouble."

"I, ah, I do *see* your point—your concern, but—"

"No 'buts,' young woman. I must insist that you remove this book—and any others like it—from the library *instantly*."

"Well—I agree with you in a way, but I don't have the—the authority to remove any book from the library. I would have to talk to Mr. Symmes about removing it from the shelves. He's the branch librarian. He's not here now, but tomorrow—"

"*I'll* be in tomorrow to talk to this Mr. Symmes myself, young woman."

"I know he'll want to—"

"This is the second time I've found bias in this library, and this time I intend on *doing* something about it."

Since the next day was Miss Lothrop's day off, she left a note on Harry Symmes' desk before leaving the branch, explaining that he might have a demanding visitor to cope with that day. She also noted the general nature of the complaint.

When she returned to work a day later, Miss Lothrop approached Symmes and inquired if the "last angry woman" had in fact come in to see him.

"You bet she did! Full of the crusade—to smite down prejudice—*and* to save her scalawag of a grandson. Say, what did *you* tell her anyway? When I sent her packing, she said that the young lady she talked with on Tuesday—you, Alice—agreed that the *Dictionary should* be off the shelves. Made it a bit awkward for me."

"I *did* agree that she had a point, Mr. Symmes, *but* I never—."

"Don't worry about it, Alice. They always do that. She was some character. Name's *Miss* Goodenough! *Miss*—get that! A grandmother a *Miss!* Told me she's a 'Lucy Stoner.' I suppose she thought Goodenough was *good* enough. Boy, what a life. Never dull, that's for sure."

"How did you get rid of her?"

"Told her—in my most sonorous tones—that to purge the records of the past of expressions which are derogatory to minority groups would be tantamount to rewriting history. Told her, too, that I'm a Jew and that I know what prejudice is all about. That got her."

"Well good for you, Mr. Symmes."

"She didn't like it much. Started going on about how we don't have any history books for teenagers in the library that give an unbiased account of the Negro's contribution to American history. You can't please them all, I suppose."

The following Monday, Symmes received a telephone call from Paul Gould, Orehard Public Library's branch supervisor.

"Harry, we've been having some trouble at central from a Miss Goodenough. Know her? Claims you have some book that's belittling to Negroes. That you don't have others which give the real picture. And that you were disrespectful to her."

"Of course I remember her, Paul. Who could forget? That voice—that little wrinkled brow. A real character. Wanted me to remove a quotation dictionary from the library because some rhymes and jingles were derogatory to colored people. I simply told her that we don't censor books at South Market or OPL. That was that, as far as I'm concerned."

"Apparently she didn't see it that way. She's tried to see Eutaw—on Friday and this morning. And she's threatening to go to the library commission. I talked with her briefly and she seems like a determined old gal."

"What's all the fuss about? We can't rewrite history, can we? That quotation dictionary—Mencken's, I think it was—that dictionary's a scholarly work. I don't see the problem. Surely, we can't go around with little rubber stamps like Hitler did—."

"Well, Harry, I don't know what transpired between you and this woman in your conversation with her, but she's shouting 'riot'—and that concerns Eutaw. And she claims that, in addition to this offensive dictionary, you don't have any material at South Market that presents the Negro case—or gives a full picture of their contributions. You know, in most textbooks, the Negro just disappears from the scene between Reconstruction and 1954."

"She did mention something, I remember, about our not having *Land of the Free*. I simply told her that because the school system decided not to use it as a text that we rejected it on the same grounds."

"You've got a good memory. I don't remember that book. A textbook, you say?"

"You don't have kids in school, Paul. I remember it being discussed at a PTA meeting. The book's OK, except it dumps on America's bad side too much. There was a big stink about it in California a few years ago."

"Well, do you have anything at South Market that gives the whole Negro story? How about the *Negro Heritage Library?*"

"I didn't order that because the reviews were so bad. It's just a bad set, that's all. But look, obviously this old bag's just a crank. I don't see what there is to get so excited about. Why the library commission wouldn't give her the time of day."

"I'm not too sure I'd agree with you, Harry. Eutaw's a pretty astute judge of these things, and he smells trouble. This woman's a crank, maybe but she's also a troublemaker—and Orehard is a racially explosive city. He's naturally concerned and when the commission meets on the seventeenth, he's going to make some recommendations about buying materials concerning racial and ethnic groups. I saw him this morning right after we got rid of this Miss Goodenough—for the second time—and he wants a policy covering such things as offensive references and how far OPL ought to go in *consciously* buying materials that put a racial or ethnic group in the best light."

"Hell's bells, Paul. I never realized this thing was *this* serious."

"Well it is. Anything to do with race in this city is—I shouldn't have to tell *you* that. What is your branch now—half Negro?"

"South Market's about half now."

"Think of the trouble we'd have on our hands if this woman were a Negro."

"You got a point—you got a real point there."

Orehard has indeed had its share of racial strife. In 1958, for example, race riots in this eastern industrial city of more than a million people rocked the country. The 1967 riots were also severe in terms of property damage. More recently, Orehard's Negro population, which totals more than 300,000, has demonstrated vociferously—and sometimes violently—for better employment opportunities, better schools, open housing, and increased recreational facilities. This restiveness among a large portion of the city's population has naturally created an acute sensitivity on the part of public officials to any incident which could possibly ignite racial feelings.

The Orehard Public Library, recognized as having fine collections and for provision of effective services, has been frequently criticized by conservative individuals and organizations in the city for its liberal selection policies. For instance, some years ago real pressure was exerted on the library to remove its copies of James Baldwin's *Another Country*; however, Robert Eutaw, director of the library, refused, and the novel remained available for adult readers. Much of Eutaw's success lies in the fact that he has managed to build an excellent working relationship over the past twelve years with the library commission, and the city council—which controls the funding of library operations.

■   Considering that the Orehard Public Library is intrinsically opposed to censorship of controversial publications, that the library subscribes to the ALA Bill of Rights and has a liberal book selection policy, and that the city of Orehard is acutely conscious of potential racial trouble, what recommendations should Eutaw make to the library commission concerning offensive references, such as those contained in Mencken's *Dictionary?* What recommendations should he make for future policy concerning "buying materials that put a racial or ethnic group in the best light?" Evaluate Symmes's attitude toward these two questions. For example, should he have purchased *Land of the Free* for the South Market Branch? *Negro Heritage Library?* Should he remove Mencken's *Dictionary* from his branch's shelves? Finally, consider Symmes's comments regarding the "rewriting" of history. What is history? How complete is the historical record? How true is it? What is the library's function in regard to it?

14
Making History

"Ah, as you both know, I wanted to, ah, to get together with you last week. But, ah, you know the bug—has no respect for the rich *or* the ah, poor." Dr. Rozella paused for a moment. "Well now. I have several items on my agenda, and, ah, then if either of you ladies have any, ah, business, it can be brought up. Ahhh—now first. There is, ah, the, ah— the matter of making certain, ah, making absolutely certain that, ah, researchers are not left alone in the, ah, Gompers room without a, ah, member of the staff being present. Manuscripts, ah, I hardly need point out, ah, to you. . . ."

Dr. Franklin Rozella, director of the Huckins Research Library on the American Labor Movement at Pender University, is an historian by training and temperament. A specialist in American labor history with a Ph.D. from a prominent midwestern university, Dr. Rozella had taught in the history department at Pender for eight years when, two years ago, a serious health problem forced him to resign his position. An acceptable teacher and a productive scholar, he has published a number of articles in historical journals and a monograph entitled *Labor Conflict on the Banks of the Monongahela,* a "reassessment" of the Homestead strike of 1892. Dr. Rozella was respected by both his students and teaching colleages, and his untimely resignation was counted as a heavy loss to Pender, especially since, at forty-six, he was still considered a relatively young man. Therefore, when the directorship of the Huckins Research Library became vacant eighteen months ago, Dr. Rozella was offered the post even though he had not completely regained his health. After debating with his wife, his doctor, and himself, Dr. Rozella finally accepted the position with the stipulation that he could not possibly devote more than twenty-five or thirty hours a week to the job.

Pender's president, who supports the Huckins Library primarily because of its prestige value to the university, agreed to Dr. Rozella's terms without hesitation, and everyone was delighted.

The Huckins Library's most important holdings consist of personal papers of prominent labor leaders and persons associated in various ways with the labor movement in this country. In some instances, the library has been fortunate enough to acquire a person's complete papers; in other cases, only isolated documents by or pertaining to some notable figure are held. For example, recently the library purchased several letters written by Eugene V. Debs, even though it does not have Debs's personal papers. In all, the library holds approximately 13,000 individual manuscript items. In addition, the library has a supporting collection of 15,000 non-circulating books and periodicals of both historical and current importance.

The major portion of Dr. Rozella's time is spent selecting and acquiring manuscript material for the library. He enjoys this work, and when he is able to snare such choice items as the Debs letters which concern the Pullman strike of 1894, long one of his passionate interests, his happiness becomes almost unscholarly. The most bothersome aspect of Dr. Rozella's job—from his standpoint—is the need to occasionally concern himself with administrative problems. He frankly admits that he has no interest in being an administrator, and that, in his own phrase, he is "not very good with people." Nevertheless, because he is a conscientious man, he tries to deal with each problem as best he can. Fortunately, for Dr. Rozella, his staff is small. Lois O'Connell, the curator of manuscripts, is chiefly responsible for cataloging new manuscript material acquired by the library. Mrs. O'Connell, who has an undergraduate degree in history as well as credits toward an advanced degree in archival work, also concerns herself with questions of manuscript preservation. Barbara Temple, the librarian, handles the selection and cataloging of the book collection, as opposed to the manuscript collection, and supplies reference assistance to researchers using the library. Mrs. Temple holds a master's degree in library science. A full-time secretary and a student assistant round out the staff.

Partially as a means of dealing with unpleasant administrative problems, such as finding the Gompers room unattended twice within the past week, and partially as a means of imparting information about new manuscript and book acquisitions and other developments of possible concern to the two professional members of the staff, Dr. Rozella now and then convenes a meeting of Mrs. O'Connell, Mrs. Temple, and himself in his office. On this afternoon, such a meeting has been in progress for about an hour.

DR. ROZELLA; "Now, ah, if there are no more, ah, questions regarding the, ah, Simbroca collection, I have, ah, completed everything on my agenda." Dr. Rozella took a bottle of large, pink pills from his desk drawer. "Pill time. Forgive me, ah, for not, ah, offering you ladies one." Satisfied that his humor had been communicated and appreciated, he gulped down a pill without the aid of water. "Well now. Do we have anything else?"

MRS. O'CONNELL: "There is something I'd like to bring up, Dr. Rozella, if you don't mind. I think the Huckins should start a tape library —along with the manuscripts. Take, for example, the Simbroca collection. Think how enriched it would be if we had Simbroca's own recollections and comments about his labor activities on tape. The letters and memorabilia don't give a complete picture for future historians. Why don't we think about instituting a program where we'd go out and tape important figures like Simbroca before they die?"

DR. ROZELLIA: "You are aware, ah, Lois, that, ah, there are research libraries which, ah, do do that sort of thing? I mean, ah, practically one of our neighbors, in fact."

MRS. O'CONNELL: "Certainly I am. I was talking to one of our researchers the other day about our *neighbor's* U.A.W. history tapes. But my point is that no one taped Simbroca even though he was very important to the teachers' union movement. We have an opportunity to use the tape recorder as an aid to historical research by accumulating material which otherwise wouldn't exist. We would be making history, so to speak. We should think of future historians."

DR. ROZELLA: "This, ah, idea is not, ah, new to me, Lois. Not new by any means. Ahhhh—oral history, as its, ah, called, was first suggested by, ah that, ah, fellow—what's his name?—Nevins! Allan Nevins at, ah, Columbia. Now then. I, ah, see our role at the, ah, Huckins as a manuscript—and, ah, book, ah, Barbara—library. I haven't used these, ah, oral history libraries, but they must, ah, be a nuisance, ah, a big nuisance to use."

MRS. TEMPLE: "May I add, Dr. Rozella, as I'm sure you know, that oral history collections are quite costly undertakings, in terms of talent, time, and—perhaps most important—money."

MRS. O'CONNELL: "I don't see what would be so *costly* about setting up twenty or thirty interviews a year with big name figures. A little extra correspondence and the effort of an hour-or-two interview. That's about it. Besides, it might be an opening to get the person's papers if we had his recollections on tape."

MRS. TEMPLE: "As I understand it, interviewing requires a great, *great* amount of preparation. The interviewer must be *completely* familiar with the background of the person being interviewed and the subject of the interview. Isn't that right, Dr. Rozella?"

DR. ROZELLA: "The, ah, interviewee and the interviewer each, ah, have their, ah, roles. They, ah—"

MRS. O'CONNELL: "All the interviewer has to do is turn on the tape recorder and let it run. It's that simple. The person talks for a few hours. That's it."

MRS. TEMPLE: "All you would get that way is a lot of rambling."

MRS. O'CONNELL: "*That's* precisely what historians *want*. It gives insights into the person's personality—how he thinks and so on. After all, Barbara, history is, among other things, an attempt to arrive at theories about human behavior by comparing what happened in the past. And what happened in the past is directly related to individual personality traits and quirks."

MRS. TEMPLE: "I think you've twisted what I meant, Lois. I can't believe that any historian would prefer to sit down and plow through someone's random, off-the-cuff reminiscences if an intelligent, well-planned interview were available. I do believe, that if you—"

DR. ROZELLA: "No, ah, Barbara—Lois is right. Ah, history is analytical and comparative. The emphasis is on, ah, man's reaction to changes in his, ah, environment through time. The, ah, only elements, ah, which separate, ah, historical inquiry from any other, ah, social science are time and the, ah, impossibility for empirical observation. Well now. The oral and visual history movement, ah, as I understand it, is, ah, an attempt to reduce the empirical limitation."

MRS. TEMPLE: "Well, Dr. Rozella, you know much more about this than either Lois or I, but isn't it true that if you're going to go to all the trouble to tape a person, you want to get the most important things he has to say? The interviewer should draw him out with well chosen questions, and not just anyone can do that."

DR. ROZELLA: "I would, ah, agree with that, ah, to a certain extent. Doubtless, the interviewer must, ah, play the role of, ah, discussion leader."

MRS. O'CONNELL: "Dr. Rozella is qualified to interview people in the labor field, I think even you would agree, Barbara."

MRS. TEMPLE: "I never suggested he wasn't. However, I doubt that he would have time to prepare for twenty or thirty interviews a year—that's one every two weeks."

MRS. O'CONNELL: "If that is the case, then cut down on the number, or I could help. I did major in history, and you pick up a lot working at the Huckins. I think what you don't seem to understand, Barbara, is that the manuscript, as we think of it, is on the way out. Tapes are needed to replace the diaries and journals that people no longer keep. Important business nowadays is transacted over the phone, and unless libraries like the Huckins tape these people, and the people they knew and worked with, *before* they die, everything is lost to the future historian."

MRS. TEMPLE: "I don't see how you can say that, Lois. Why, more documents and correspondence are being produced now than ever before. I remember reading about the problem William Shirer had going through the tons and tons of documents when he was researching the *Rise and Fall of the Third Reich*."

DR. ROZELLA: "That's, ah, true only in that, ah, official correspondence and documents are, ah, increasing. The, ah, typewriter has increased their, ah, number, but, ah, the telephone, as, ah, Lois, says, has reduced their importance."

MRS. TEMPLE: "All that may be true—I'm sure it is. But I still don't think the Huckins can afford to get involved in an oral history program. Who, for example, would do the editing and indexing of the tapescripts? That's another big job which requires a labor specialization."

DR. ROZELLA: "Oh, ah, you wouldn't want to fool with the taped interview. My, my. Why that is, ah, primary source material, just as is, ah, a manuscript. Of course, I, ah, would not deny that, ah, manuscripts have been, ah, known to be tampered with on occasion—"

MRS. TEMPLE: "Are you sure, Dr. Rozella? I think I've read where it's standard practice to submit tapescripts—the transcript of the interview—to the person interviewed so that he can correct factual errors and change grammatical mistakes and so on."

MRS. O'CONNELL: "That's completely false. I don't know *where* you read that—probably in some *library* periodical—but it's just not true. The original tape *is*, in effect, the manuscript!"

MRS. TEMPLE: "I hate to disagree with you, Lois, but that's the way it's done elsewhere, I'm sure. And, along these same lines, it may interest you to know that some oral history librarians don't even save the tape—the actual tape—after the tapescript is made."

MRS. O'CONNELL: "I'm sure that they're oral history librarians who don't know what they're doing. Why, as Dr. Rozella said, the *way* something is said is *very* important to the historian."

If Dr. Rozella had not stepped in and promised Mrs. O'Connell that he would look into her suggestion for setting up an oral history program at the Huckins Library, it is possible that the discussion may have continued on and on. "As, ah, I said previously, I'm a, ah, manuscript man myself, but, ah, there is no harm, I suppose, in, ah, entertaining the idea of, ah—how did you, ah, put it, Lois?—of making history."

■ After investigating the literature pertaining to oral history, analyze the discussion which took place in Dr. Rozella's office, and attempt to determine the validity of each participant's position. Consider, for example, the question of who should conduct the oral history interview? What are the interviewer's role and responsibilities? How are oral history tapes used by scholars? Is preservation of original interview tapes important, as both Dr. Rozella and Mrs. O'Connell firmly suggest? Does the interviewee usually have the opportunity to correct the tapescript of his interview? How much indexing of tapescripts is required? Approximately how much money would it take to organize and administer an oral history program at the Huckins Research Library? Finally, would you recommend that Huckins should start "making history?"

15

No Piggy Deals

As if a nasty head cold and a flat tire on the way to the library were not enough for one morning, Elton Marsh was having a difficult time concentrating on his correspondence because of interruptions by one telephone call after another. As his telephone rang again, Marsh, director of the Social Science Division of the Midland State University Library, switched off his Dictaphone and muttered to himself, "Goddamn phone—."

"Professor Bradlee calling for you, Mr. Marsh."

"Thanks, Jane. Put him on." Marsh replied as cheerfully as possible. Bruno Bradlee, an associate professor of political science, was one of the few faculty members at Midland whom Marsh knew socially as well as professionally. Both men, who were in their late thirties, shared an interest in national and local politics which, perhaps more than any other single reason, accounted for their friendship.

"Good morning, Bruno. How's the body politic?"

"Morning, El. Appropriate question. Did you happen to catch the Hard-nosed Representative Mr. Joel Franklin Messinger on channel eleven last night?"

"No, I didn't. I went to bed early last night. Was he on—what's it called—?"

"Legislative Line Up. You should have seen him tearing into the governor and his new budget. Good ole Hard Money Messinger!"

"Messinger's tough as nails and twice as conservative, no question about that. I'm really—"

"Sounds like you have a cold, El."

"A beaut. It's in full-bloom this morning. At least I can't give it to you over the phone. But go ahead—fill me in on my least favorite state representative."

"Well, besides being ugly as ever, the old pol introduced me to some new terminology. Said that just as another friend of the poor had once called for 'No Piggy Deals in Washington,' he was launching a campaign for 'No Budget Deals in the Statehouse.' Now what in hell are these 'Piggy Deals'?"

" 'Piggy Deals'?—Afraid I must confess ignorance on that one, Bruno."

"In the context of his tub-thumping diatribe, he seemed to imply that these 'Piggy Deals' were illegal or corrupt or, at least, immoral. I looked the phrase up in my copy of Smith and Zurcher's *Dictionary* without any luck. I thought maybe you'd be able to find out. As a political science professor, I *ought* to be familiar with references like that. No doubt some wiseacre will bring it up in class tomorrow. It's not all that important, but I *am* curious. Would you mind checking around in some of your sources, El?"

"Be glad to. You've got me interested, too."

"I thought, in a wild moment, of calling Messinger's office but, hell, that would probably give him more ammunition to use against the university —pinks, queers, eggheads, peaceniks. You know his line."

"OK, Bruno. I've got to get back to a mountain of correspondence. I'll look this up and give you a call later today. How's that?"

"Sure, that's fine. There's really no hurry about it, although I would like to be prepared for that potential wiseacre."

"Are you at home today?"

"Will be until three o'clock. Working on the book."

After a brief conversation about Bradlee's progress on his book, Marsh concluded the call by assuring Bradlee that he would attend to the "Piggy Deals" matter at once. Whereupon, he contacted Sarah McLean, the senior member of the division's reference staff, and explained Professor Bradlee's question to her. "Aside from the meaning of the phrase, he'd probably like to know a bit about who used it, too. This shouldn't take more than a minute or two, Miss McLean. Probably in one of the political dictionaries."

Midland State University is one of the most important state universities in the country. With a current enrollment of approximately 26,000 graduate and undergraduate students and a faculty and staff in excess of 7,000, the university maintains three suburban centers in addition to the main campus. Founded in 1871, as a result of the Land Grant College Act of

1862, Midland has grown from a student body of thirty-five in its initial year of operation to its present size as a result of careful administration and generous financial support—Representative Messinger notwithstanding—from the state legislature.

Likewise, the university library is outstanding in terms of both size and quality. With over 3,500,000 volumes listed in its union catalog, it is one of the largest state university libraries in the nation. Dedicated as the Jacob Henry Hayes Memorial Library three years ago, the new central library has integrated most of the departmental libraries which were previously scattered around the campus, although the schools of agriculture, aviation, medicine, and pharmacy still maintain separate library collections. The central library is organized on broad subject departmental lines. The Social Science Division, for example, covers the fields of economics, political science, sociology, and anthropology. While responsibility for acquisition of specialized reference materials and maintenance of subject reference service is in the hands of each subject division, a general reference collection located on the first floor of the building houses the major trade bibliographies, a wide range of general fact-finding tools, and the printed catalogs of such libraries as the Bibliotheque Nationale, the British Museum, and the Library of Congress.

Miss McLean, a forty-five year old woman of stolid disposition, came to Midland nine years ago. After working in the cataloging department for six or seven months, she joined the reference staff of the Social Science Division and has worked there ever since. During Elton Marsh's two years as director of the division, Miss McLean has gained his confidence as a competent, though somewhat unimaginative, reference librarian. At four o'clock, soon after Marsh had returned from his afternoon coffee break, Miss McLean appeared in his office, reporting that "Piggy Deals" had eluded the lexicographers.

"Mr. Marsh, I checked all our dictionaries that list political terms, like *Dunner* and *Plano and Greenberg*. I even looked in *Smith and Zurcher*, even though I think you said that Professor Bradlee had checked it himself. I learned something about 'Pigeonholing' but nothing about 'Piggy Deals'."

"Did you try any historical sources—*Dictionary of American History, Morris, Carruth?*"

"Yes, Mr. Marsh, I did. I checked ours, and then I trooped over to the History Division. I thought I ought to do it personally, since it's for Professor Bradlee. I even looked in Kane's *Facts About the Presidents*."

"Well, it must mean something, or Representative Messinger wouldn't have used it."

"I even looked in some of our British political dictionaries, even though I can't imagine a Britisher using a word like 'piggy'."

"All right, Miss McLean. Tomorrow morning I'll see what I can do with it. Just give me a list of the sources you've already checked."

"Mr. Marsh, couldn't we call the state capitol and ask the man himself?"

"I toyed with that idea myself, but I think that we have to remember that Messinger has no love for the university, and a call from me to his office *just* might be something he'd make an issue of. We better let sleeping dogs lie."

That evening, Marsh made a point of checking the newspaper for coverage of Representative Messinger's remarks. Indeed, there was a story, on page three, which summarized the lawmaker's fiery comments and quoted the "No Budget Deals" statement—but no mention was made of pigs.

■   Keeping in mind Miss McLean's futile efforts to uncover the author and meaning of "No Piggy Deals in Washington," how would you proceed if you were Marsh? Compile a list of sources, other than those noted in the case, which Miss McLean probably consulted or should have consulted. What is the answer to Professor Bradlee's question?

16

Investing For Small Capitalists

Eight months have passed since Rita Copeland was appointed to the position of librarian in the community of Tetlow, a white-collar suburb located in one of the largest metropolitan areas in the country. Miss Copeland's predecessor, Miss McBride, an elderly woman who enjoyed clipping the local newspaper and searching out-of-print catalogs for exotic cookbooks (Tetlow Public Library, the *ALA Directory* notes, has a special collection of American and foreign cookbooks), finally retired at the age of seventy-four after more than thirty-five years as the director of the library. Directly out of library school, Miss Copeland has attempted to bring a degree of both innovation and professionalism to the Tetlow Public Library—neither of which had concerned Miss McBride unduly. And, by and large, she has been successful in her efforts thus far.

The library's board of trustees, relieved to have found a replacement for Miss McBride with a minimum of trouble, has cooperated fully with Miss Copeland, agreeing to such initiatives as replacing the manual charging system with a mechanical one, and redefining certain staff positions and duty assignments. Initially, Miss Copeland had been somewhat timorous of making changes in library procedures on her own authority, soliciting instead advice from her board. She quickly discovered, however, that the trustees had little interest in or knowledge of day-to-day library operations and were quite content to let her have a free hand. This point was driven home to her when, after a few months on the job, she requested that the board approve her suggestion to eliminate the practice of permitting a local book jobber to bring selected samples of new fiction to the library for the purpose of selection, apparently, as far as Miss Copeland could learn, the only method of choosing current novels employed by Miss McBride for many years. The trustees, much to Miss Copeland's surprise, professed ignorance of this long-standing routine, and indicated that she could continue or abandon it as she saw fit. From that time on, Miss Copeland informed the board of her decisions rather than asking its permission.

Soon after her arrival, Miss Copeland began an intensive evaluation and weeding of the collection, finding as she progressed that the library's holdings were deficient in many areas. Not only did great gaps exist in the small collection, but much of the material on the shelves was sadly dated. Especially was this true in the fields of business and economics, where the only books in the library of any value were several current best sellers and a few popularizations such as Heilbroner's *Worldly Philosophers* and Burton Crane's *Getting and Spending*. On the other hand, the library contained nothing by A.A. Berle, J.K. Galbraith (Miss Copeland immediately ordered *American Capitalism, The Affluent Society,* and *The New Industrial State*), or Veblen—to name but a few respected economists not represented in the Tetlow Public Library. The general reference collection was in a similar state of neglect, many of the approximately a thousand volumes useless because of their age. Miss Copeland estimated, after making some rough calculations, that nearly one-fourth of the library's 45,000 books would have to be discarded eventually. Since her book budget, $14,000 annually, was below minimum standards at the present time, she knew that serious retrospective buying would be out of the question, at least for a year or two.

One afternoon, Miss Copeland was busy preparing her first annual budget for submission to the board of trustees (this was one subject in which each member seemed to be vitally interested) when Ted Sidlaw, the president of Tetlow's Chamber of Commerce, dropped in for a "chat." After complimenting Miss Copeland on her good works during the past several months ("Dandy little machine you've put in to stamp the books"), Sidlaw got to the real point of his visit.

"You know, Rita, the Chamber has almost 40 members—merchants, businessmen—who have businesses either on the 'belt' or right in Tetlow. And we're growing all the time. Now for years—years—we tried to get old Maggie McBride to break down and get some investment sources in the library."

"I know we don't have much along that line, Ted, but—well—"

"Much! Nothing is more like it. Why, you know some of us small capitalists in the Chamber who occasionally put an extra buck into investment enterprises have to go over to Glenhill to use *Moody's Manuals?* That's a fact."

"I agree that it doesn't seem fair that you people have to drive eight or nine miles just to use facilities which ought to be here, but the budget—"

"I say this, Rita—and I used to say it to old Maggie—if Glenhill can have *Moody's Manuals,* why can't Tetlow?" Ted wrinkled up his nose, the picture of disdain.

"What did she say?"

"No dice. Cookbooks first." He grinned, seeing that the inference had not been lost on Miss Copeland. "I'll tell you this, Rita. If you could get *Moody's Manuals* here at Tetlow, I'll betcha I could get the boys to kick in with a little money for other things along that line. You know, a gift to the library now and then. The Chamber'd be behind you one hundred percent, believe me. After all, Tetlow's not just any burg—we're twenty thousand happy, prosperous people."

"Well, Ted, my budget's tight enough as it is—as you can guess. There's so much the library needs. But I do have a few hundred dollars left from the current budget which I have to spend before June 30th. I've been so busy finding out what we need that I haven't been spending what I have fast enough. And, frankly, I'd just as soon spend this money on some large purchase to clear the books—to get the bill by the end of June. I was thinking of the *Oxford English Dictionary,* but maybe *Moody's Manuals* would be more useful."

"You think about it, Rita. And, remember, ONE HUNDRED PER-CENT!"

Miss Copeland did think about *Moody's Manuals* and the following day decided to order the five volume service. Before making the decision, she checked the reference and periodical holdings in the library for business. Her survey showed that the Tetlow Public Library owned the following reference tools: Clark and Gottfried's *Dictionary of Business and Finance,* Munn's *Encyclopedia of Banking and Finance* (1964 edition), an old volume of *Economic Almanac, Poor's Register of Directors and Executives* (latest edition), *Handbook of Basic Economic Statistics* (current annual volume), and *Thomas' Register of American Manufacturers* for 1963. Even more dismal was Tetlow's periodical collection. The library subscribed to only four periodicals (selected, Miss Copeland decided, because of their inclusion in the *Reader's Guide to Periodical Lit-*

erature, the only periodical index purchased by the library) which may be useful to patrons interested in the business world: *Business Week, Fortune, Consumer Reports,* and *Changing Times.* The library also subscribed to the *Wall Street Journal.*

The following week, at the regular meeting of the library's board of trustees, Miss Copeland presented a number of items of business, the most important being her budgetary requests for the coming fiscal year. She casually mentioned, too, the fact that *Moody's Manuals,* a popular five volume business service, had been ordered and would soon be available on the reference shelf. The board made no comment on this particular announcement, treating it as a routine matter.

Several days later, however, Miss Copeland received a telephone call from the chairman of the board of trustees, Dorothy Croydon, who told Miss Copeland that her husband did not think that *Moody's Manuals* was the best service the library could have purchased.

"Jim's with Herbert, Hopkins, Quint, Parley, and Oaksquare in the city and they often use things like *Moody's.* When I told him we were going to have *Moody's* in the library here, he said that it's certainly not the best service available. There's others he says that are better."

"Well, Mrs. Croydon, I studied *Moody's Manuals* in library school and I believe it's an authoritative service. Which one does your husband think we should have bought?"

"I'm sorry, but I don't remember exactly what Jim said they were called. One was F and S something or other. And is there one called Standard and Poor something? However—I must say that I was unaware *completely* of the cost of this *Moody's.* Jim says it must have cost over *four* hundred dollars."

"I think, though, Mrs. Croydon, it will be worth it in the long run. After all, Tetlow has a lot of businessmen and local investors who need the kind of current business information *Moody's Manuals* give."

"Nevertheless, Miss Copeland, in light of the cost I believe the board should discuss this purchase at our next meeting. Will you place that on the agenda for the meeting on the tenth?"

Miss Copeland indicated that she would do that and ended the conversation by telling Mrs. Croydon that she would be most happy to discuss her decision with the trustees at the next meeting.

■ Compare *Moody's Manual of Investments—American and Foreign* with other similar investment services, defending or rejecting Miss Copeland's decision on the basis of that comparison. Knowing what you do of the Tetlow Public Library, consider if the purchase of *any* investment service is justified at the present time. What other pertinent reference materials in the business field could be purchased for the price of *Moody's* or a competing service? Should Miss Copeland consider establishing a reference service for local businessmen sometime in the future? What are the library's obligations to this special group?

17
Matters Military

"Does the library have any other books on European history, other than the ones over there, Mrs. Elwyn?"

Paula Elwyn, librarian at Champney Township High School, rearranged the 3x5 cards in her hand. It was a few minutes before two o'clock and the final period of classes had just begun. "Why I don't believe so, Carol. Are you looking for one you can't find? Maybe it's checked out. What is the title?"

"No special one, Mrs. Elwyn. Only I need to find out if all the European countries ever served under one general, and I've been through the books over there." She pointed toward the books shelved in the 900 classification.

"I'm not sure I follow you, Carol. All the countries of Europe under one flag? If that's what you mean, NATO must be the answer. One general is over them all. Is this for Mr. Zamora's European history course?"

"That's right—Modern European History. But NATO couldn't be it, because Russia's not a member of NATO."

"Perhaps, Carol, Russia is counted as an Asian country."

"Well, it's not in Mr. Zamora's class. We study about Russia. We're reading *To the Finland Station* now.

"I see."

"Are there any other books in the library I could look in? I looked in all those over there and in the *Rise of Modern Europe* books Mr. Zamora taught us about."

"Let me think. Why don't you try the *Encyclopaedia Britannica?* That's certainly one of the best encyclopedias for European history."

"OK, I will on your say so, Mrs. Elwyn, but Mr. Zamora won't like it."

"What do you mean? Why won't he like it?"

"Well! Mr. Zamora is *very* strict about our using the encyclopedia. He says it's a crutch and that we should learn to use books and other reference things."

"Well, why don't you try the *Britannica* anyway, this once. After all, what you really want is the answer."

"OK, Mrs. Elwyn. Thanks."

Champney Township High School, located in a predominatly agricultural area of one of the eastern states, enrolls close to 900 students. Serving a radius of approximately 15 miles, the consolidated high school was opened in 1964. In 1968, an additional wing of classrooms was constructed to alleviate overcrowding. About 20 percent of Champney's students eventually go on for some kind of higher education.

The high school library, organized during Champney's first year of operation, was set up by Mrs. Elwyn's predecessor, a Miss Hull. Containing about 10,000 volumes, including a basic reference collection which was selected from basic lists and faculty suggestions by Miss Hull, the library is used extensively as a study area by students during school hours. Mrs. Elwyn came to Champney in September, 1966 on a provisional basis following Miss Hull's resignation. Although she had worked for a few years before her marriage in the circulation department of a large public library, Mrs. Elwyn has no professional library training and, for this reason, she offered to take the position only until a qualified librarian could be found—and she has been on the job ever since. Her husband teaches biology at Champney.

"Mrs. Elwyn. I looked all through the encyclopedia and I can't find anything. And now it's almost time for the period to end and then I got to catch my bus. And I *got* to know by tomorrow second period or Mr. Zamora will bawl me out."

"Now, now, Carol, don't get in a state. Can't you get to the public library tonight?"

"Oh, Mrs. Elwyn, I live too far out. And anyway, Esty's library is no good."

"I didn't know you live out Esty way. You must know the Custers."

"My Mother does. I only have five minutes left. Isn't there some other place I can look?"

"What about your textbook?"

"Oh, the answer to Mr. Zamora's questions are never in the book. See, he wants us to learn to look other places. And, anyway, we hardly ever use the book. We use paperbacks. Like I said, we're reading *To the Finland Station* now. It's an advanced course—for college prep."

"Well, Carol, you run along. I'll have a look in my reference books and you come in tomorrow right after the bus arrives and I'll see if I can have the answer for you."

"Gee, you're a pal, Mrs. Elwyn. I gotta go now—thanks *awfully*. Thanks. Bye."

Mrs. Elwyn left a student helper in charge of the library, which remained open until four o'clock to accommodate those students who live in the immediate vicinity, and walked down the long first floor corridor to Mr. Zamora's room.

"Hello, Ernie. Am I glad I was able to catch you."

"Hi there, Paula. How's things in the library?" Ernie Zamora continued stuffing papers in his briefcase. "Excuse me, but I'm in a bit of a rush tonight. Dentist appointment. Ugh." He made a face. "Then Joan and I have to hotfoot it over to Leedsville for the game. You and Harry going?"

"I don't think we'll make it tonight. I don't want to keep you, but it's about little Carol Bussey. Apparently she has some assignment about finding out if the countries of Europe were ever under one flag? Is that right?"

"Under one flag? Under one—oh, sure. I see. Sure, sure. I give little research questions as you probably know and, as I recall, Carol is to report on the circumstances that led to the one and only time in modern history when all the great powers of Europe served under a single military commander."

"I see."

"I'm pleased to hear my students are using the library. I tell them to be sure and ask you if they can't find what they're looking for."

Mrs. Elwyn flushed slightly. "Well, as a matter of fact, I really am helping Carol. She couldn't stay since her bus was leaving and I offered to help her with the question—."

"She's had that assignment for a week. But I'm sure with your help there'll be no problem. Lord, the time! I have to run. Nice to see you, Paula. Drop by again when I don't have the dentist breathing down my neck—or better, get Harry to bring you over to Leedsville tonight."

Mrs. Elwyn returned to the library and began looking over the reference collection for sources which may be useful for questions concerning European history. Aside from the multivolume series *The Rise of Modern Europe* (edited by William Langer) which Carol had already investigated, Langer's *Encyclopedia of World History*, the *New Cambridge Modern History*, and *The New Larned History for Ready Reference, Reading, and Research* appeared to be the only obvious sources in the collection.

■ Will the "obvious" fact-finding tools which Mrs. Elwyn has available be sufficient to answer the student's question? What other less obvious sources might conceivably be found in Mrs. Elwyn's reference collection? When researching this problem, pay particular attention to indexes of the tools used, noting strengths and limitations.

18
The Balancing Act

Old Harbor is a New England community of 19,000 people. The scenic coastal harbor, an important element in the original settlement of Old Harbor in 1657, no longer plays a significant part in the community's economic life, although its quiet, natural beauty does attract a certain number of tourists each summer from around the country. Most of the town's work force is engaged in manufacturing of one type or another—the latest figures available show that 204 firms and businesses, most of them small, employ nearly 8,000 persons. Private education also contributes to the economy of Old Harbor, with a junior college and two private academies supplying jobs for teachers and other staff who live in the community and outlying areas.

In 1964, Old Harbor built a new public library after two years of bitter wrangling over its proposed architectural style. A dull building of simple red brick, which visitors sometimes mistake for the post office, was finally constructed, suiting no one entirely but offending only those who had opposed any building at all. The town librarian, Adelaide Rand, had pushed for a building with some "verve" but in the end she reluctantly went along with the majority of the town selectmen who accepted the plans which resulted in the present building.

Miss Rand, a white-haired woman in her mid-fifties who has lived in Old Harbor for most of her adult life, has been director of the library for over 15 years. She had taught English at Durland Academy in Old Harbor for a number of years before leaving, in the words of one town wag, "under hasty and peculiar circumstances" to attend library school where she earned a master's degree in library science. Several years later, she returned to Old Harbor as the town librarian. Over the years, Miss Rand has earned the respect of the reading public in Old Harbor as a knowledgeable and helpful librarian. Her only public idiosyncrasy—keeping her dog, a wirehaired fox terrier named Group Captain, in her office at the library while she works—is considered by most townsfolk to be a sign of healthy individualism.

The library's financial support is adequate in light of ALA minimum standards, with an operating budget of something over $80,000, of which approximately $16,000 is spent on books and periodicals. Until 1964, when the new building was completed, Old Harbor Public Library did not have a professional reference librarian, Miss Rand feeling that the demand for information in the community did not warrant such an expenditure. However, when library use increased steadily after the new building was occupied, she changed her mind. And when the library's first reference librarian resigned several months ago, Miss Rand immediately advertised the position in national library periodicals, apparently convinced that there was a real need for this kind of service in Old Harbor. The advertisements produced two likely prospects, with the job finally going to Gerald Dwinell. Dwinell, who had taken both his graduate and undergraduate degrees at a large university in California, told Miss Rand during a telephone interview that he felt that his one year's experience in a municipal library in California qualified him for the Old Harbor position. She agreed and, after consultation with the library committee, Dwinell was hired.

Dwinell had been working at Old Harbor Public for a week or two when Miss Rand asked him to drop by her office, "just to talk about the new job and get better acquainted." After inquiring about Dwinell's new living quarters, bus routes, and the accessibility of shopping centers, Miss Rand asked how he was getting along at the library.

"Fine. Just fine. Everyone on the staff is very helpful. Very pleasant."

"I know, Mr. Dwinell, that you have not, as yet, had time to *completely* familiarize yourself with all our operations, but I am very anxious to have your suggestions. Procedures, policies—anything at all. We're a small staff, but, I believe, a sound one. I'm so happy you like them, by the way. I think *they* like you, too. And improvement of service is always necessary, so I do hope you will always feel *completely* free to make suggestions. I have guarded against complacency all my life in a personal way and I *do* hope I do the same for OHPL."

"I'm flattered, Miss Rand, to know you want any ideas I have. Frankly, I like what I see so far. The reference collection needs a good weed, perhaps, but that's about all."

"Oh, *really*. Mrs. Mather, our former reference librarian—she left, as I believe I told you, to take a school library position so her hours would conform to those of her children's—Mrs. Mather was *very* conscientious. But your fresh ideas will be welcome—*certainly* welcome."

"I enjoy the—well hello there, pooch." Group Captain had jumped onto Dwinell's lap and was licking his face.

"Get *down*, Group Captain. *Bad, bad* boy." The dog obeyed. "I *am* sorry, Mr. Dwinell. His manners. But he *does* so love people."

"That's all right. I like dogs."

"Now where were we? You were saying something."

"I was just going to say that I enjoy the book selection part of my job here, too. In my only other library job—in California—I didn't have any kind of authority and it was a bit galling to see the mispractices that took place. For example, there was no attempt at balance at all."

"Balance? You mean balance between fiction and nonfiction?"

"Not exactly. I mean ideological balance."

"That kind of balance—if I follow you—*is* most difficult to achieve. I'm not even sure it can be done—not sure at all."

"It's my belief, Miss Rand, that it can be done—and must be done. Balance of controversial views is necessary and, I think, it's the library's job to see that that balance is fostered. The library must be absolutely neutral ideologically."

"You're saying, I take it, that *each* book for patriotism must be balanced by one against it—for religion or democracy by one against it? That seems like so much bunkum to me, Mr. Dwinell. And please don't be offended by my direct language—it's an old New England custom." Miss Rand smiled.

"That's not *quite* what I mean. It's been well established, I think, that the most influential reviewing journals, such as *The New York Times Book Review, Book World, Saturday Review,* the *Atlantic*—let's see—the *New York Review of Books, Booklist, Library Journal,* that these reviewing journals have a 'liberal' bias, and this as such acts as censorship against certain books, since most librarians only select from reviews."

"*What,* Mr. Dwinell, would you use to *balance* the publications you have just mentioned?"

"Well, after I'm more familiar with the ins-and-outs of my job, I want to start getting the *American Legion Magazine*—which I'm very surprised we don't get now—and things like the *Dan Smoot Report, Modern Age,* the *Manion Forum, Combat, Counter-attack, Human Events, American*

Opinion, the *Freedman*—journals that represent the other side of the coin to supplement the job the *National Review* does. Not all these review books, I know, but they keep you up on significant titles. For example, *Smoot* has footnotes—"

"I am *very* wary of some of those publications—others, I admit, I have not heard of. And, I am wary of *that* approach to book selection, Mr. Dwinell. We are commissioned by Old Harbor to select books on the basis of their individual worth, not on their ability to balance other books in the collection. In fact, I am *not* convinced that this ideological neutrality you speak of is a good thing. Perhaps libraries ought to have a point of view occasionally, if for no other reason than to avoid mass think."

"That's why—"

"Let me finish please—then it will be *your* turn. Now Old Harbor *is* a conservative community. Almost seventy percent of the voters went Republican in the last election. If I understand you, you are saying that books of a conservative philosophy are not reviewed in *The New York Times* and so on. I am unaware of any study that may have been done on the subject, but I *rather* think that you will find that *The Times does* review books of all political views. Certainly we have few complaints at the library."

"I don't know of any studies, either, but it's been my experience that if the liberal journals do review books they don't agree with, they condemn them out-of-hand. Look what they did with Jim Burnham's *Suicide of the West* a few years ago or his *Web of Subversion*—or Ralph Toledano's *Greatest Plot in History.* Others, as I said, don't get reviewed anywhere. For example, we don't have Teixeira's *Fabric of Terror* here—I checked. The reason, I bet, is that it wasn't reviewed. Stang's *It's Very Simple* is another case in point. I would have missed that one if I'd only been using the liberal journals. Fortunately, I learned about it through reading *Smoot* or *Manion.* I think I picked up Teixeira's book through the *Liberty Letter.* In fact, all the liberal reviewers shy away from controversial books of any kind, not just political ones. Guy Endore's *Satan's Saint* is a good example."

"What is this *Liberty Letter* you mentioned?"

"It's published by the Liberty Lobby, a group in Washington which tries to influence legislation. You'll be surprised to hear that it has—or had—a larger circulation than either *Human Events* or the *National Review.* It's published monthly and mainly it urges readers to write to their congressmen on important issues."

"You are *certainly* up on this, Mr. Dwinell. However, getting back to your original point, are you not forgetting that in order to properly balance a collection, each item would *necessarily* need to be labeled? Not only political opinion, but everything else as well."

"I don't agree that labeling is necessary at all. Let people make up their own minds. Just look at the periodical collections in most libraries— Old Harbor included. You find the same old magazines that are on sale at the supermarket. Instead of buying the safe things, which are those usually produced by the liberal press, we should present the other side, too."

"My goodness! Do you know we have talked right into my luncheon engagement. Mr. Dwinell, I want to let you know how provocative this has been. I *do* want to give a bit more thought to this balance business and then, sometime soon, let's get together and discuss it further. *And,* I would like you to give it some more thought also—then you can let *me* know if you still think we need the *Liberty Letter* here at OHPL."

■   Assess the arguments concerning balance of book collections presented by Miss Rand. By Dwinell. Is Miss Rand, for example, correct when she states that the major reviewing journals do, in fact, review books of all political viewpoints? Is she right when she states that a properly balanced collection would *necessarily* entail labeling? Is Dwinell correct in saying that the major reviewing journals are inclined toward a "liberal" point of view? Is he right when he implies that conscious balance in collection building, in all areas, is necessary in the public library? Comment on Dwinell's assumption that the *National Review, American Opinion,* the *Manion Forum,* and similar periodicals of a conservative persuasion can effectively balance the *New York Times Book Review, Library Journal,* etc. Finally, consider the question of ideological neutrality vis-á-vis the role of the public library in this country.

19
A Man's World?

While Ingleside Woman's College is primarily known in educational circles for its humanities program—well over 50 percent of the 940 girls currently attending the college are working toward a bachelor of arts degree in either fine arts or literature—undergraduate professional training in the fields of business, education, and publication is also available. The professional "schools," as they are called at Ingleside, are comparatively recent additions to the college's academic program, the result of a calculated attempt, begun a decade ago, to diversify the curriculum and appeal to a wider range of potential students. At the present time, approximately 260 girls are enrolled in the three professional programs, and all indications suggest that this number will increase in the future. Located in one of the larger industrial states in the eastern section of the country, Ingleside was founded in 1844 by the Methodist Church "to provide a Christian interpretation of all fields of learning." Today, the college's Methodist affiliation is nominal rather than substantive. A Phi Beta Kappa chapter was established at Ingleside in 1922.

Ingleside's library development, quite naturally, has followed curricular development. Traditionally strong in humanities subjects, in recent years the library has steadily and rapidly expanded its collections in business, education, and publication. The college librarian, Josephine Fowler, reports that total holdings now number 167,532 volumes, with approximately 5,000 volumes being added annually. Periodical and newspaper subscriptions are placed at 875. The library employs a staff of 15, eight of whom are professionally trained. In addition, there is the usual corps of part-time student assistants. The library's largest problem at the moment concerns faculty members who insist on taking books and periodicals from the library and keeping them indefinitely in their offices, creating what Miss Fowler has called "scattered, informal departmental libraries." Officially, no departmental collections exist, except for the School of Publication's small clipping and radio and television tape library.

Mary Roach was just finishing her coffee in the faculty lounge when Theodore Valentine, director of the School of Publication, tapped her on the shoulder. Miss Roach, an Ingleside alumna (1958), worked for several years in a large university library in the New York area after completing her library degree and then returned to Ingleside as head of reference services in 1962. The position, which carries faculty status, is demanding and requires considerably more time than the officially designated 35 hours a week. To encourage a good working relationship with both students and faculty, Miss Roach spends 20 or 25 hours a week at the public reference desk. She believes that too few professional librarians have enough actual contact with their public, and she was determined that this would not be the case at Ingleside, at least while she was there. In keeping with this philosophy, Miss Roach has instituted a non-credit course at Ingleside called "Research Methods and Sources," which has proved to be surprisingly popular with students.

"Mary! Just the gal I want to see—have another cup."

"I really shouldn't, Val. Duty calls."

"Stay here. Don't move." In a few seconds, Valentine returned with two cups of coffee. "I put cream in yours—that all right?"

"Fine. Now, Val, what did you want to see me about?"

"The School of Publication has received a modest grant from the Flavia Foundation, and I've been—"

"What is the Flavia Foundation?"

"A small, private foundation interested in journalism. It makes a number of grants each year to individuals and organizations—unsolicited. The money can be used for any purpose, as long as it promotes journalism in some way."

"No strings?"

"No strings. Nice, no? Now—I've been casting around for something to do with our money and I thought it would be reasonable to sponsor a small study on women in television writing. Harriet is going to make up a questionnaire, but first we'll need a bibliography. We'll have to know what's been done sooner or later. What I wanted to know is, will you do it? I don't have the time and neither does Harriet or Jane. We'll pay you by the hour—whatever you think is a fair rate for your professional services."

"Why, Val, I'll do this literature search for nothing. It's part of my job."

"We have the money, Mary. You may as well get some of it—that's what the grant's for. Make it six or seven dollars an hour."

"All right, if you put it that way, Val. Now—how soon will you need the bibliography?"

"No rush. Say a month? Mid-December?"

"Fine. That's plenty of time. Now—the subject—I'd better write this down—the subject is women in television work?"

"Women in television *writing*. Just writing."

"All types of TV writing?"

"Anything that deals with women in television writing. Opportunities, types of jobs, career information, numbers employed—anything. But don't bother with general books on television writing. For example, there's no need to include something like Roberts' *Television Writing and Selling*— unless there's a special section on women."

During the next several weeks, Miss Roach worked on the *Women in Television Writing* bibliography during slack periods at the reference desk and, occasionally, on her lunch hour. A few days before the agreed upon deadline, she gave a brief bibliography of 16 items, along with a list of the sources she had checked (*see* Appendix), to Valentine's secretary. In addition, she included a bill for $90 and a note explaining that she had used 1950 as an arbitrary cutoff date when conducting the search, and that she was mildly surprised by the lack of material on the subject.

The following day, Valentine called Miss Roach and thanked her for her efforts. However, he had reservations about the thoroughness of her work.

"Only fifteen or sixteen references! I really feel sure that you-you've missed a lot of material—important books and articles. I'll admit not *much* is published on women in television writing, but there *must* be more than fifteen or sixteen references. That's about six dollars a reference. Come on, Mary, who do you think you're kidding?"

Astounded by Valentine's attitude, Miss Roach went to Miss Fowler and told her the story—betwixt sobs and tears. Miss Fowler, who was a sympathetic but strict administrator, listened without a word until Miss Roach had finished, and then told her that she should forget about Valentine's harsh words and judgment.

"He'll get over it. I know Val a lot better than you do. He'll have forgotten all about it in a week's time. What disturbs me more, however, is that you were doing this project for money—on college time. I would strongly question the ethics of that, Mary. When you're feeling better, I'd like to talk to you about it."

■   Criticize the list of sources Miss Roach used in her literature search (*see* Appendix). What important bibliographic tools has she failed to consult? Who is right about the amount of published material on the subject of women in television writing: the subject expert relying on his memory, or the librarian relying on her bibliographic aids? Or could they both be right? In your opinion, can a bibliography of only sixteen entries on this subject be justified?

Appendix

Reference Sources Searched for the Compilation of the Bibliography

Besterman, Theodore. *A World Bibliography of Bibliographies.* 4th ed. revised. Geneva: Societas Bibliographica, 1965-67. 4v.
Bibliographic Index; A Cumulative Bibliography of Bibliographies. New York: Wilson, 1937- to date.
Broadcasting Yearbook. "Books and Reference Works for Radio and Television," 1950- to date.
Broderick, Gertrude G. *Radio and Television Bibliography.* Washington: Government Printing office, 1956.
Cumulative Book Index; A World List of Books in the English Language. New York: Wilson, 1949- to date.
Dissertation Abstracts. Ann Arbor, Michigan: University Microfilms, 1950- to date.
Essay and General Literature Index. New York: Wilson, 1948- to date.
Hamill, Patricia Beall. *Radio and TV, Selected Bibliography.* Washington: Government Printing Office, 1960.
Ingleside Woman's College. Library Catalog.
———. School of Publication. Clipping File.
Journal of Broadcasting. "Graduate Theses and Dissertations on Broadcasting," 1956-to date.
Journalism Quarterly. "Report on Graduate Research in Journalism and Communication," 1950- to date. (Title of this annual feature varies from 1950 to the present.)
Price, Warren C. *The Literature of Journalism: An Annotated Bibliography.* Minneapolis: University of Minnesota, 1959.
Public Affairs Information Service. *Bulletin.* New York: Public Affairs Information Service, Inc., 1950- to date.
Readers' Guide to Periodical Literature. New York: Wilson, 1950- to date.

Social Science and Humanities Index. New York: Wilson, 1950- to date. (Formerly *International Index.*)

Subject Guide to Books in Print; An Index to the Publishers' Trade List Annual. New York: Bowker, latest edition.

U.S. Superintendent of Documents. *United States Government Publications: Monthly Catalog.* Washington: Government Printing office, 1950- to date.

Vertical File Index. New York: Wilson, 1950- to date.

20 / On Admissions And Mental Illness

As soon as he had finished speaking with Dean Vinson, Mark Seaver dialed his secretary's number. "Martha, is Mrs. Rice in the office at the moment?"

"No, I'm sorry, Mr. Seaver. She's scheduled at the reference desk until twelve-thirty, when she goes to lunch."

Seaver glanced at his watch. "OK, thanks."

After clearing his desk of several miscellaneous papers, Seaver, the director of the Halls College Library, left his office and walked down a flight of stairs to the main floor of the library where he found Patricia Rice, the college reference librarian, seated at the reference desk. He exchanged greetings with Mrs. Rice and then got directly to the point.

"Pat, I've just had a call from Dean Vinson in the admissions office. She'd like us to supply some information if we can, but wants the nature of it kept confidential." Seaver, who had seated himself opposite Mrs. Rice at the desk, unbuttoned his suit jacket.

"Even though I'm a woman, Mr. Seaver, I promise not to talk. Seriously, though, I can keep a secret and I'll regard the Dean's request with strictest confidence."

"Good. Now the Dean is anxious to have us find any information—particularly statistical information—we can on admission of high school students to college who have a history of mental illness. Apparently, Halls has a policy of non-admission if an applicant has ever been hospitalized for psychiatric reasons or has undergone any kind of psychotherapy."

"I didn't know that."

"Neither did I—until the Dean told me. In confidence, I should add.

At any rate, she's just come back from a professional meeting somewhere and, apparently, she was discussing the subject with some other admissions people. Now she's thinking about asking the faculty committee on admissions to reconsider our policy, but, naturally, she wants to study the matter thoroughly before she makes a recommendation."

"Could you be a bit more specific, Mr. Seaver? Does she want to have us find out what other colleges do? Or what?"

"No. I gathered from my conversation with her that she wants some idea of how many applicants with a history of mental problems are accepted by colleges—and universities, of course—around the country each year in spite of their psychiatric problems. And how many are rejected on the same basis. And also how those who are accepted fare. Do they flunk out? Become honor students? Just what happens to them? Or anything else that's relevant. Clear?"

"Yes. That gives me a better picture of what she wants."

"I doubt if this kind of information is publicized by individual colleges, anyway. According to the Dean, this subject has been taboo in educational circles, but I don't doubt that she could, if she wanted to, call some of her professional counterparts in the area and informally find out how they handle this problem."

"Cass and Birnbaum's *Comparative Guide* may give that kind of information—I'm not sure."

"Well, if it does, I'm sure the Dean would appreciate knowing about it —but I rather doubt that it does." Seaver re-buttoned his jacket as he stood up. "As you're probably aware, Pat, Gloria Vinson has not always been the library's greatest booster, so I think it's important that we give her request as much time as we can. And get it to her relatively quickly. I hope you'll be able to devote some time to this this afternoon."

"I'm not scheduled at the desk this afternoon—except to relieve Rose for coffee. I was going to catch up on interlibrary loans, but that can wait."

"Good. I'm going to be tied up the rest of the day and most of tomorrow, so I'd appreciate it if you could take charge of this and draft a memo to the Dean as soon as you've come up with enough information. Just give it to Martha to type—and ask her to type it over my signature. I think under the circumstances that that would be best in this case."

After lunch, Mrs. Rice began working on Dean Vinson's request by heading a blank piece of paper "Admissions Procedures Pertaining to Applicants for College Who have Suffered from Mental Illness." Then she compiled a list of possible reference sources to consult: Cass and Birn-baum's *Comparative Guide to American Colleges; Education Index; U.S. Office of Education's Statistics of Education in the United States; Encyclopedia of Educational Research; College Blue Book;* and *Dissertation Abstracts.* As an afterthought, she also jotted down the acronym ERIC.

■   Halls College is a small, independent liberal arts college for men and women which has earned a substantial national reputation for academic quality during the 125 years of its existence. In 1965, the college opened a new, three-story air-conditioned library which houses a well chosen collection of some 110,000 volumes. The solution to this case involves constructing a memorandum addressed to Dean Vinson which will satisfy her request for information in a responsive yet expeditious manner. In addition, consider Mrs. Rice's list of reference sources to be checked in terms of 1) the most effective and efficient order in which to consult them; 2) the utility of each source apropos of the information sought; and 3) other reference tools which could, or should, be added to her list.

21

The Mayor And His War On Hooliganism

"Good morning, Mr. Flint. Have you seen the *Burley Sentinel* this morning?"

"No, Betty, can't say that I have. Avoid the sheet like the plague. You know *The Times* is the only paper—all the news that's fit to print and all that." John Flint, reference librarian at the Burley Public Library, emptied his briefcase onto his desk, habitually his way of beginning the work day.

"I'll bet—just bet—*The Times* doesn't have the story on our Mayor."

"You may—just may—have something there, Betty. Burley would need the birth of quints plus the Mayor for a coup like that. OK, OK, let's see the *Sentinel*. As a public-spirited public servant, I suppose I owe it to the community to keep up with the Mayor's political career. Who's he browbeating today?"

Betty Carey, an assistant in Flint's department, gave the paper to him with a you'll-be-surprised smile, pointing to the front page headline.

MAYOR PALFREY'S HOME HIT BY VANDALISM— YOUTHS BLAMED

By Paul Rutland

Early this morning, Mayor Richard C. Palfrey's residence at 45 Turner Road was the object of a paint-throwing incident, presumed to be the work of youthful vandals. In addition to splattering the Mayor's house with gallons of various colored house paint, the vandals did extensive damage to recently landscaped shrubbery. Police theorize that teenage vandals are responsible for property damage estimated at $3,000.

Police Chief Elmer Cross, who has taken personal charge of the investigation, called the attack "an outrageous act of juvenile violence which the city could not tolerate."

Chief Cross said that orange, red, green, and yellow paint was splashed on all sides of the house. "Apparently they just stood back and heaved," he said. Two birdbaths were also defaced, it was re-

Continued on Page 4, Column 3

The story, Flint had to admit to Betty, was an interesting one indeed. Although he did not know the Mayor personally, Flint was familiar enough with stories concerning Palfrey's zest for relentlessly vanquishing political opponents and local committee chairmen to realize that the Mayor would not rest until the culprits were found and punished. Certain sections of Burley, sure enough, were accustomed to patchy occurrences of teenage vandalism, but Turner Road was definitely not one of these.

Later, at lunch, Lincoln Nyack, director of the public library, commented to Flint that the story was the talk of Burley. According to Nyack's information, Jim Driske, editor of the *Sentinel,* was planning a tough editorial condemning the unfortunate episode as an insult to the entire city and its good name; political wits were now referring to the Mayor's house as "Burley's aurora borealis;" and butchers, barbers, and curbstone lawyers found the story a refreshingly "colorful" topic of conversation. "I'll bet you this, Lincoln," Flint remarked over his apple pie, "that he won't take it lying down. Every cop on the force will be on this one."

The following morning, John Flint had scarcely begun to empty his briefcase when the library intercom buzzed. "Good morning. Flint speaking."

"Good morning, John. Lincoln. I just called to congratulate you."

"Morning. What do you mean—congratulate me? A raise in salary maybe?"

"You were absolutely right about the way Palfrey's reacting to that little paint job. He's hopping mad. And I mean *mad.*"

"Probably heard about the aurora borealis remark. He's not investigating you, is he?"

"No, nothing quite that dramatic, John. But he has been in contact with me. Could you come up to my office sometime this morning to talk about this thing? Seems Palfrey wants some materials on juvenile delinquency."

"Well, well. How about that. The crusade begins, of all places, in the library."

"Say about eleven, John?"

At eleven o'clock, John Flint appeared in Nyack's office and learned that late the preceding day Mayor Palfrey had telephoned the library to inform Nyack that a committee to study juvenile delinquency in Burley was being appointed. Explaining that while this problem had naturally concerned him for quite sometime, recent outbreaks of "hooliganism" in the city had forced him to the conclusion that the time for bold action had finally come. The Mayor further explained that his action plan would be two-pronged: in addition to appointing a blue-ribbon committee charged with investigating the causes and effects of delinquency and eventually recommending possible long-range solutions, immediate steps were being considered to, in the Mayor's words, "get the little bastards off the streets." After inviting Nyack to serve on the committee, the Mayor requested that the library "round up some books and things on delinquency so that the committee can get going and not just sit on its ass."

"Of course, John, I told the Mayor that I'd be more than delighted to serve on the committee and that the library would be willing to compile a bibliography of pertinent books, articles, reports, and so forth, and have it ready for the first meeting, which will be a week from tomorrow."

"He moves fast—you have to give him that. Just glad I'm not one of Burley's hooligans."

"Right. Now I'm hoping, John, that you'll be able to take on this job of compiling a bibliography. I know you're pretty busy with the business project, but I'd like the library to really impress the Mayor by showing him what we can do. You know, he's been pretty decent about library appropriations. And this could also result in some good public relations for the library with the rest of the members of the committee."

"Who's on the committee, besides you?"

"Paul Dunboy. Hal Cleveland—a school committeeman. And, of course, superintendent Gill. Bob Mangano of the Youth Club. Let's see, who else? Oh yes—two clergymen. Father Galen and Reverend French. I believe Palfrey also mentioned that Ted Chandler of Fabricated Metals may be a member. And there may be several others besides the Mayor and myself."

"Well, I'll give this project top priority this week. How exhaustive do you think the list of titles should be, Lincoln?"

"John, you know as much about it as I do at this point. I think you'll just have to use your own judgment as to what might be useful to an *ad hoc* group studying juvenile delinquency in Burley. I am hoping that you'll be able to come up with some studies that other communities have conducted—community action programs and so forth. Two other things do occur to me. Palfrey specifically asked for any information we have or could get on curfews—"

"Curfews??"

"That's right. I hope Palfrey doesn't have in mind what I think he does. I tried to draw him out, but he was pretty guarded."

"I'll try to find something which shows that curfews don't work."

"Remember, John, we'll have to be fair about this."

"I was only kidding." Flint grinned.

"The other thing is federal programs or money available to communities like Burley for preventing and controlling delinquency. I don't know, but probably HUD or HEW or the Labor Department have programs for direct or indirect aid. I doubt if we could get anything, but trying wouldn't hurt."

"Sounds reasonable."

"Yes, and one other thing. Would you recommend one or two titles that could possibly serve as background for the committee, so that I can have multiple copies ordered for the committee? A book that generally introduces all aspects of juvenile delinquency."

"General bibliography for background. Curfews. Federal assistance. And a book which gives an overview. OK, Lincoln, I'll try to have this to you several days before your first meeting. I may give Coker a buzz at the college and find out what they have that's useful. I know he has *Sociological Abstracts,* for example."

"That's all right, John, but don't involve anyone over there in this. Palfrey's not especially friendly toward them."

Burley, a city of 95,000, is located in one of the Middle Atlantic states. Not an ostentatiously wealthy community, Burley does have a sizable number of light industries which have consistently flourished during the last ten years, thus keeping the per capita income somewhat higher than the national average. Because Burley's geographical situation is not particularly attractive—the nearest metropolitan center is almost 150 miles away—it has been industry again which has accounted for the slight growth in population over the last decade; semi-skilled and skilled workers have been attracted to Burley in sufficient numbers to offset the increased movement of the white-collar middle class to small towns just outside the city. Although several ethnic groups contribute to Burley's population profile, ghetto-like conditions have not developed to any alarming extent.

Municipal services are adequately supported, and Mayor Palfrey, now in his third two-year term as the city's chief executive, has been particularly concerned with improving the public school system and, to a lesser extent, the public library. Under Lincoln Nyack's direction for the past four years, the library has kept pace with the general improvement of library service which has taken place throughout the state during the period since 1960.

Coming to the Burley Public Library nearly two years ago directly from library school, John Flint has concentrated on increasing reference service to business and industry in the city. The reference collection contains most of the current fact-finding and bibliographic materials likely to be found in a medium-sized public library, and Flint's budget for new acquisitions compares favorably with American Library Association recommendations as set forth in the current edition of *Minimum Standards for Public Library Systems.*

In addition to a small, lackluster business college of 360 students located in the heart of downtown Burley, a liberal arts college of over 800 students of some regional repute is situated near the outskirts of the city.

As he had promised, John Flint had a bibliography dealing with juvenile delinquency on Nyack's desk several days before the first meeting of the Mayor's Study Committee on Juvenile Delinquency, as it was now officially known. At his first opportunity, Nyack looked over the typewritten bibliography which Flint had prepared. First he read a memorandum attached to the bibliography.

To: LRN
From: JAF

Here it is! I can obtain photocopies of any articles included. And most of the books either we have or I can borrow from Coker at the College library.

I recommend the Committee use *Juvenile Delinquency; a Book of Readings,* edited by Rose Giallombardo (Wiley, 1966). It's available in paper and offers the best overall survey of the subject to come along in years. As an alternative, you may want to use *Juvenile*

Delinquency in American Society (Harper, 1961) by Harry M. Shulman. It's excellent—but a bit dated. Both are erudite and would give the Committee a perspective of causes, effects, and possible solutions.

As far as community action programs for prevention and control of JD go, there isn't much available. The federal government has put out a few pamphlets which are listed in the bibliography, but those I examined did not seem very helpful. The best source for this kind of information is Powers and Witmer's *Experiment in the Prevention of Juvenile Delinquency* which is also listed. This is the old Cambridge-Somerville, Mass., youth study. Since it was published in 1951, it probably won't be terribly useful.

As far as I could determine, the federal government does not give money to individual communities for JD prevention, although the Department of Labor does maintain several training and research programs. It might be worthwhile for the committee to write the Department for information.

There is nothing in the literature about curfews (honest!), at least not in the sources I searched. If you want, I will continue looking, although I think I have covered the major comprehensive bibliographic sources.

Sources searched:

1) *Education Index.* 1950-
2) London School of Economics and Political Science. *Bibliography of the Social Sciences.* to date.
3) *Psychological Abstracts.* 1950-
4) *Sociological Abstracts.* 1952-
5) UNESCO. *International Bibliography of Sociology.* 1952-
6) Card Catalogs. Burley Public and Gaffney College.

JOHN

Lincoln Nyack frowned and studied the first page of Flint's bibliography (*see* Appendix) with some care. He then scanned the remaining pages of the bibliography at random. Dissatisfied, Nyack determined to see Flint as soon as possible. Three full working days remained until the committee meeting, and Nyack hoped that it was still possible to have a usable bibliography ready by that time.

■ If you were Lincoln Nyack, what specific criticisms would you make to Flint regarding his bibliography, assuming that page one given in the Appendix is representative of the entire list? In the course of the literature search, has Flint neglected to search any important bibliographic sources? How do you react to Flint's claim that he has "covered the major comprehensive bibliographic sources?" How would you organize a similar literature search? Do you concur that Rose Gaillombardo's *Juvenile Delinquency* is the "best overall survey" available? Comment on Flint's conclusions about the quantity of material available on specific community programs to prevent and control juvenile delinquency; about federal activities in this area; about curfews as a means of control.

Appendix

Page One of John Flint's Bibliography for the Mayor's Committee

Ackerman, Nathan W. "Adolescent Problems: a Symptom of Family Disorder," *Family Process*, I (September, 1962), 202-13.

Adelson, Joseph. "The Mystique of Adolescence," *Psychiatry*, XXVII (February, 1964), 1-5.

Ball, J., Alan Ross, and Alice Simpson. "Incidence and Estimated Prevalence of Recorded Delinquency in a Metropolitan Area," *American Sociological Review*, XXIX (February, 1964), 90-92.

Barron, Milton L. *The Juvenile in Delinquent Society*. Alfred A. Knopf, Inc., 1955.

Berner, Peter and Walter Sprel. "A Special Type of Autistic Juvenile Delinquency," *Journal of Offender Therapy*, VI (May, 1962), 18-19.

Block, Herbert A. and Arthur Niederhoffer. *The Gang*. Philosophical Library, Inc., 1958. (Chapters 16 and 17 should be especially useful).

Bowerman, Charles E. and Glen H. Elder, Jr. "Variations in Adolescent Perception of Family Power Structure," *American Sociological Review*, XXIX (August, 1964), 551-67.

Brown, Roscoe C., Jr. and Dan W. Dodson. "The Effectiveness of a Boys' Club in Reducing Delinquency," *Annals of the American Academy of Political and Social Science*, No. 322 (March, 1959), 47-52. (Other chapters useful also).

Burchill, G.W. *Work-Study Programs for Alienated Youth; a Casebook*. Chicago: Science Research Associates, Inc., 1963.

Burt, Cyril. *The Young Delinquent*. 4th ed. London: University of London Press Limited, 1945.

Clark, John P. and Edward W. Haurek. "Age and Sex Roles of Adolescents and their Involvement in Misconduct: a Reappraisal," *Sociology and Social Research*, L (July, 1966), 496-508.

Clinard, Marshall and A.L. Wade. "Toward the Delineation of Vandalism as a Sub-type in Juvenile Delinquency," *Journal of Criminal Law, Criminology, and Police Science,* XLIII (January-February, 1958), 493-99.

Cloward, Richard A. and Lloyd E. Ohlin. *Delinquency and Opportunity: a Theory of Delinquent Gangs.* Glencoe: The Free Press, 1960.

Cohen, Albert K. *Delinquent Boys: the Culture of the Gang.* Glencoe: The Free Press, 1955.

———. *Deviance and Control.* Prentice-Hall, Inc., 1966. (Chapter 8 should be useful).

Cooke, Paul. "Delinquency Prevention through Educational Intervention," *Journal of Negro Education,* XXXV (Spring, 1966), 151-60. (This article, though in a Negro journal, is general enough to be useful).

22

Burley In Transition

Mayor Palfrey's war on juvenile delinquency continued to attract considerable attention in Burley, even though the unfortunate paint-throwing episode had occurred weeks ago and the culprits had yet to be caught and brought to justice. Particularly controversial was the City Council's recent imposition of a 9:00 evening curfew on all children sixteen years old and younger, a "temporary" measure proposed and urged by the Mayor until his *ad hoc* Study Committee could "make recommendations of a more permanent nature to alleviate the growing problem of juvenile delinquency in Burley." Much to the Mayor's surprise—and pleasure—instituting the curfew resulted in substantial statewide radio, television, and newspaper publicity. Most gratifying to the Mayor personally was his lengthy telephone interview with a reporter representing the largest daily newspaper in the state capital. Certainly, not all editorial reaction to the curfew was laudatory—the perjorative "Victorian" cropped up more than once—yet the majority of comments the Mayor had heard or seen commended the idea as a forceful, pragmatic approach to a difficult social problem. Besides, Palfrey—a politician —knew that the first rule of both political survival and ambition was to be talked about. What was said mattered, but that *something* was said mattered more. Each morning, as he shaved, Mayor Richard Charles Palfrey wondered if perchance he was looking at the face of a future governor.

Since the twelve-member Mayor's Study Committee on Juvenile Delinquency was appointed some two months ago, it had met twice in the Mayor's office at City Hall. At the first meeting, the Mayor recounted his longtime concern with the vexatious problem of "hooliganism" in Burley, announced his plan to ask the City Council for a "temporary, but indefinite", evening curfew for teenagers, and suggested that the Committee begin immediately to study the delinquency question so that it could recommend possible long-range solutions within the next six months or so. T. Roland (Tommy) Gill, school superintendent, was designated chairman of the Committee, and Father Galen volunteered to act as secretary. After a mimeographed bibliography of readings on juvenile delinquency and paperback copies of Kvaraceus's *Anxious Youth* (Merrill, 1966) were distributed to each Committee member by Lincoln Nyack, city librarian, the meeting adjourned for coffee and doughnuts, compliments of the host. The second meeting was marked by bickering on the part of several Committee members about questions of procedure, the merits of the now operative curfew, and some of Kvaraceus's ideas regarding juvenile delinquents. The need for a self-study survey apropos the Committee's work was discussed, and a subcommittee consisting of Nyack, chairman, Councilman Dunboy, and Bob Mangano of the Youth Club was appointed to explore the idea and report back at the next meeting. Finally, a decision was made not to request funds for an outside consultant to advise the Committee, after Mayor Palfrey noted that public money was not available for such purposes, and that he believed the Committee did not need "some outsider telling us what to do."

About ten days before the next scheduled Committee meeting, Lincoln Nyack received a telephone call from Mayor Palfrey. The Mayor, usually buoyant these days, sounded defensive and irritated.

"Look, Linc, I got a letter here. From some sociologist professor up at Tonawanda by the name of Grayson. He heard about my curfew and wants to come down here to get 'basic social facts' or some goddamn thing."

"What—about juvenile delinquency in Burley?"

"Something like that. Hell, I can hardly tell from this letter. Why don't those bastards just speak plain English. Look, Linc, I'm not a naturally suspicious guy—you know that—but this bird wants to come down here with a mess of people and snoop around. Interviewing people. Poking in records over here, probably."

"Sounds as if he wants to do a social survey of Burley."

"You're goddamn right he does. And as the mayor, I can't allow this city to get a black eye like that."

"What do you mean, Dick? A black eye?"

"Come on, you've heard about these surveys. Jesus Christ, you've probably got some in the library. They dig up dirt on a town and then broadcast it around. People get all upset. They go in and find out a few kids are using marijuana or something and the whole town gets it. We got some fine publicity from the curfew, but this would hurt us all. Probably say the library's no goddamn good, either."

"Well, thinking back to my college sociology course, I can't remember that Duluth, or Muncie, or wherever it was, suffered too much from the famous Middletown surveys. The Lynds' surveys."

"I don't know. Maybe they didn't. Maybe they did. Look, Linc, I got to get the hell off this phone. I'm sending a copy of this letter over to you. I want your committee—that sub-committee—to answer the damn thing. Tell this bird we're doing our own survey. I'd answer the goddamn thing myself, but—it'll look better coming from you. I talked to Tommy Gill and he agrees."

"But maybe this professor could be of some use to us—"

"Look, Linc—"

"—since we don't know the first thing about conducting a survey."

"You can learn. You got the books over there, don't you? Or should— the budget's high enough. All you got to do is ask the kids why they're fooling around and what they'd rather be doing. Talk to parents. Keep it all in the family."

"Well, if this professor from Tonawanda wants to survey Burley, we can't stop him, that's obvious."

"Ha! I can and I will."

"Wait a minute, Dick. Since we're going to have to get into this survey business one way or another, why not let me find out more about how they're conducted? What they accomplish? What methods they use? Send me the letter, and I'll try to evaluate what the professor's survey would entail. We can write for clarification if something isn't clear. There's no hurry about answering his letter, is there?"

"It'll keep for awhile."

"Well, why not? We can't lose anything by looking into it, can we?"

"Hell, I guess not. But keep the lid on this. When we tell the bastard where to go, I don't want it all over the place that I'm anti-intellectual or against professors."

The following morning, Nyack received a copy of Professor Grayson's letter to Mayor Palfrey.

Tonawanda University
College of Social Science
125 East Seventh Street
Tonawanda

Department of Sociology   November 13, 19—

Richard C. Palfrey
Mayor
City Hall
Burley

Dear Mayor Palfrey:

It is with very real interest that I have been following your current efforts to effect controls over the pathological phenomenon of juvenile delinquency in Burley. The increasing rise of disaffection among youth and its resultant effects upon the societal fabric are of particular concern to sociologists, psychologists, and other social scientists, as well as civic and political leaders like yourself.

Since viable solutions to delinquent behavior are of more than casual exigency, and hinge on development of accurate predictive devices, I have been engaged for the past two years, in association with Dr. Horace Chipman, Assistant Professor of Psychology, a colleague here at Tonawanda, in formulating prognostic tables designed to discriminate between delinquent and non-delinquent attitudes and behavioral attitudes and behavior patterns among middleclass youths. Specifically, we are seeking through a series of studies to test Hathaway and Monachesi's hypothesis, i.e., deviant personalities reveal a proneness to delinquent behavior, on middle-class youths by introducing different variables and utilizing a wider range of methodological procedures.

Our procedures include use of projective techniques such as the Rorschach tests, picture tests, thematic apperception tests, picture-frustration studies, and similar devices. These are followed up with the traditional non-directive interview, questionnaire, and life history methods of collecting case data. Unstructured stimulus situations, valuable as they are for ascertaining beliefs, attitudes, feelings, and underlying motivations, are limited in that measurement techniques remain somewhat unreliable. Of course, Dr. Chipman and I use a variety of supporting methodological procedures, mainly statistical and ecological which utilize basic social data from census and local sources.

Such investigations naturally require the active support and cooperation of local officials and unimpeded access to local records, particularly
juvenile court and police records and data accumulated by the school
department. Because of your demonstrated concern with the problem of
delinquent behavior, both Dr. Chipman and I are hopeful that you and
other municipal officials will welcome a Tonawanda University sponsored
study of juvenile delinquency in Burley. We estimate that such a study
will require approximately six months field work for data collection and
evaluation. At various times, up to eight student field workers may be
involved in this aspect of the inquiry.

I shall, therefore, hope to hear from you in the near future concerning
the possibilities of a Burley survey, as outlined above. While I have
every confidence that your response will be enthusiastic, I hope that you
will feel quite free to contact me at the University if questions about
the nature or substance of the study should occur to you.

Sincerely yours,
Arthur J. Grayson, Ph.D.
Associate Professor

■ This case involves an analysis and evaluation of basic principles
and methodological procedures pertaining to social research. After fa-
miliarizing yourself with the historical development, characteristics, and
problems of social research, consider the following questions related to
the case situation: What kind of social study would be most useful to the
Mayor's Committee, i.e., what does the Committee need to know about
juvenile delinquency in Burley? What methodological problems will the
Committee encounter if it attempts a self-study? How would you go
about organizing such a study? What methodological procedures would
you recommend be used? From the limited information presented in Dr.
Grayson's letter to Mayor Palfrey, do you believe the proposed Tonawanda study would be useful to the Committee? Why? How would you
assess Grayson's proposed study? Is the methodology sound? How does
it differ from that used by Stark Hathaway and Elio Monachesi in their
predictive study cited by Grayson? Is Mayor Palfrey's reaction to Grayson's proposal typical? Reasonable? Is Nyack's reference to the Middletown surveys correct? How much cooperation does the social researcher

require when undertaking a survey or community study? What larger questions concerning social and behavioral research are implicit in this case situation? For example, how does the laboratory of the social scientist differ from that of the physical or biological scientist? What effect does this have upon the social scientist's relationship with the politician, who is responsible for solving social problems?

23
The Over-Psychoanalyzed Society

Nearly everyone who knew him had remarked at one time or another that Professor Maxwell Harrishof certainly looked like the stereotyped Hollywood characterization of a college professor. Along with a remarkably complete repertoire of stock professorial facial expressions ranging from the classic knitted-brow-pensive to the winsome open-faced-comprehending, Maxwell Harrishof had graying temples, was tall with only a dignified trace of scholars' stoop, and, of course, he smoked a pipe. Moreover, those who knew him best had said at one time or another, if only to themselves, that Max not only physically resembled the popular image of the professor but that indeed his behavior fit the pattern, too.

Every academic institution has its share of prima donnas, and Harrishof outshown all others in this category at Worley College. A man of enormous vanity and dogmatic hauteur who professed to value the Inquiring Mind above all else while his actions suggested otherwise, Professor Harrishof frequently exasperated students, colleagues, and Worley administrators alike. On the other hand, over the years he had cultivated a number of essentially harmless and amusing eccentricities which served to counteract the worst effects of his egotism and intellectual intolerance. For example, there was his adamant refusal to study for a doctorate. As a younger man beginning his teaching career at Worley, he had ridiculed the Ph.D. as a "farcical ritual not dissimilar to a primitive tribal ceremony designed to propitiate evil spirits." More recently, however, as his position in the psychology department at Worley became secure and his ability to professionally compete in his field was demonstrated, Harrishof began to tell those who wondered at his academic qualifications that there was no one in psychology with whom he could profitably study. "Who could test me? I'm in the same position as that Shakespeare fellow at Yale was some years ago. He *was* the authority—who could test him?" Harrishof said this with a wink, but he was not completely joking.

Because of poses like this, and because he drove a 1939 LaSalle coupe, was popular with factions of the student body, wore outré neckties, was an excellent raconteur, talked seditious nonsense at faculty meetings, was a bachelor, therefore useful as an "extra man" at social affairs, and was generally considered to be Worley's most accomplished intellectual gadfly, the Worley academic community both cherished and tolerated Maxwell Harrishof, M.S. Besides, he occasionally produced an article for a psychology journal, and several years ago he was asked to deliver a paper at a national professional meeting—all of which went a long way toward helping to rationalize Max's limitations, particularly with the college administration. In fact, some wondered why a man of his abilities and proven distinction remained buried at Worley, a small college which was neither academically or geographically anywhere.

Rodney Parker, reference librarian at Worley, was helping a student find material on poverty programs at the card catalog when he noticed Max Harrishof sitting by the reference desk, presumably waiting for Parker to finish with the student. Parker enjoyed talking with Max, finding him witty, intelligent, and usually prepared to indulge in a bit of campus gossip. Leaving the student with an admonition not to forget to check the periodical indexes he had mentioned, Parker walked over to his desk and greeted the professor.

"Max. What's new? Where have you been keeping yourself?"

"There you are, Rodney, old boy. Where have I been? Working, writing, teaching, talking to that colossal ass Dabney. Same old routine."

"Discussing the play with Dabney?"

"What else? You saw it. Disastrous, wasn't it? Absolutely an insult. Why *must* colleges try to do Tennessee Williams when they have *Our Town* talent? You tell me."

"You're right, Max. It stank."

"Absolutely and utterly without dimension or depth. And that *girl*— that Beverly what's-her-name. I told Dabney exactly what I thought."

"Apparently he didn't learn anything from the Beckett flop last year."

"Dabney is beyond learning—the man's simply an ass. A colossal ass.

But I did not come over here to discuss Dabney, old boy. I need your professional services about a small matter."

"Anything, Max—if you'll give me that tie you've got on. I thought I'd seen them all." Parker laughed.

"This tie? It's new—my last trip to New York. Reminds me of Miró. Same exhilarating use of color—bold and childlike. No, Rodney, you stick with your paislies. They enhance your complexion."

"OK, I'll stick. Now what can I do for you professionally?"

"Somewhere, sometime ago, I read about a study which was conducted of behavior at cocktail parties—an utterly useless bit of research. It tried to determine at what stage of intoxication the imbibers began to lay lighted cigarettes on the piano or started to set sweating glasses on uncovered furniture and so on and so forth."

"Might be interesting to housewives who give parties."

"Can you see grown men running around doing that. Hiding behind livingroom draperies. I've looked through my journals at home, but I couldn't run across it."

"And you want me to find this study?"

"I would be most grateful. Think of it as a contribution to scholarship, Rodney, old boy. A group of psychologists, bless them, have invited me to address a meeting next month, and I've decided to use an article I've been working on as the basis of the speech."

"What's this speech on—drinking habits?"

"That article is tentatively entitled 'The Over-Psychoanalyzed Society'—"

"You're still on the Szasz kick?"

"Rodney, sometimes you disappoint me. Like most people with a course or two in psychology you're brainwashed into believing that psychologists have all the answers—that all this highfalutin research is of the greatest moment. Dr. Szasz has quite conclusively shown that psychiatry aspires to the same pretensions."

"But you're not a psychiatrist—"

"I'm a *psychologist*, old boy, and damned pleased to be one, thank you very much. That doesn't mean that Dr. Szasz isn't right about his conclusions. I may remind you that he is a psychiatrist." Harrishof knocked out his pipe in Parker's wastebasket. He could never remember that smoking was not permitted in the library.

"Well what's the point?"

"Clear as that odd nose on your face, old boy. Too much research—or so-called research—in psychology is meaningless and pretentious. These fellows will study anything, just as Szasz has shown that members of his profession confuse 'mental illness' with problems arising from the stress of modern living."

"And you want this study on drinking as an example of useless research?"

"Rodney, you're emerging from the cave of darkness. I was reading over my article last evening and I found that, for a live audience, I need a very funny example of just how ludicrous this kind of behavioral research can get. A bit of dark humor to reinforce the point."

"Negative reinforcement?"

"Rodney, please. Don't get me off onto Skinner. I said *reinforcement* —period."

■ Attempt to comply with Professor Harrishof's request and locate the study of behavior at cocktail parties. What bibliographic tools will be most appropriate to search? In what sequence? Do you agree with Harrishof that much research in the field of psychology, and presumably other behavioral sciences, is pretentious and meaningless? For example, what value might a study of cocktail party behavior have? For whom?

24 / Amerasians

The Malverna Public Library serves not only a rapidly growing western city of 145,000 but it also provides library service for much of Malverna County with a population of 96,000, excluding Malverna, through a network of branches, book stations, and two bookmobiles. The new air-conditioned central library, now nearly two years old, replaced an unattractive, increasingly inadequate Carnegie building which had functioned as the city's main library since 1901. Leo Carlow, director of the library, came to Malverna six years ago and immediately began pressing for a new building by dramatizing—sometimes quite spectacularly—the severe limitations of the antiquated Carnegie structure. Since the completion of the new central library, Carlow has given priority to strengthening nonfiction collections in order to counterbalance the library's traditional emphasis on supplying fiction. According to the most recent annual report, the system's total book collection now stands at 279,000 volumes, including bound periodicals.

By 9:15 A.M., Sandra Minks, one of Malverna's two full-time bookmobile librarians, had completed her preparations for the Belmore route—circulation records were in order, requested books were alphabetized and placed on the proper shelf, and the children's collection had been stocked with fresh titles. Mr. Craft, the driver, indicated that he would be "ready to roll" in 15 or 20 minutes. Glancing at her watch, Miss Minks hurried to the reference area, hoping to find Susan Jenner, head of general reference at Malverna.

"Hi Paula. Is Miss Jenner around?"

"Hi Sandy. She's in the office—or was a few minutes ago."

"Thanks." Miss Minks entered the small office and found Miss Jenner looking through a stack of cards.

"Good morning, Sandra. Not on the bookmobile today?"

"Oh yes—we're leaving in a few minutes. Belmore today, so I have a little time. It's the short run. I hate to bother you so early in the morning—"

"That's perfectly all right. I was on a bookmobile for a year or so myself once—when I was at Rockwood—and I know how difficult it is to take care of business at central. You're always missing the people you need to see."

"It *is* a bit difficult sometimes, as you say. What I wanted to see you about was a reference question I received yesterday—in Wendell. I've filled out the ref card, but I thought I ought to see you personally, since it's a bit out of the ordinary."

"Yes?" Miss Jenner took the card which Miss Minks handed her and began to look at it.

"Mrs. Cordis—the patron—was very shy about asking, but I think I finally got what she wants to know." Miss Minks blushed slightly.

" 'Information pertaining to illegitimate children of American soldiers in Asia. How many such children are there? What usually happens to them? How many are adopted by Americans and brought to the U.S. to live? Can paternal grandparents adopt the illegitimate child if their son does not marry the girl? Do marriages between American soldiers and Asian girls usually succeed?' I suppose that's clear enough, Sandra, but isn't this a question for a government agency—probably the immigration authority?"

"That's what I thought, but Mrs. Cordis doesn't want to get involved with government or army officials. She's not very well educated, but an awfully sweet woman. I've gotten to know her pretty well since I've been on the bookmobile, and that's probably why she asked me."

"Do you have any idea why she wants this information?"

"Well, she didn't say exactly—and I really didn't ask. But I do know that she has a son stationed in Korea. I guess it may have something to do with him, maybe."

"Is this woman—this Mrs. Cordis—in any hurry for the information?"

"I told her I'd try to have something by next Wednesday—that's when we get to Wendell again. I hope we can help her, Miss Jenner. She seemed—well—sad."

After Sandra Minks departed, Miss Jenner asked Paula Hooker, a reference assistant, to work on the Cordis question when she had time that morning. "Sandra's reference card indicates that she has checked

Statesman's Yearbook, Statistical Abstracts, and *Collier's Encyclopedia,* sources she has on the bookmobile. What I'd like you to do, Paula, is check our catalog and *Books in Print* for any titles that seem relevant. Then check some sociology sources such as *Sociological Almanac, Encyclopedia of Social Work, Social Science and Humanities Index,* the UNESCO bibliography. You might even try *Sociological Abstracts,* even though we only have it since 1963. Use your own discretion and imagination. We should be able to find some information, particularly on the last part of the question, but I'll probably have to contact some government agency about the adoption questions. Would you let me know how far you have progressed with it before you leave for lunch?"

■ Because the Malverna Public Library is the largest library within a radius of 80 miles, and because Susan Jenner is a highly capable and interested reference librarian, Malverna has developed a strong, well-balanced reference collection. Obviously, in attempting to answer the multi-faceted question asked by Mrs. Cordis, no single source will be sufficient. Consider, therefore, which sources will be most useful for each part of the question. Criticize the list of sources which Miss Jenner suggested to Paula Hooker. What important sources of information did she fail to mention which the library may have? Is it likely that the library will have information about "the adoption questions," or is Miss Jenner correct in her assumption that she will have to contact a governmental agency? Prepare a detailed answer for Mrs. Cordis's question from sources likely to be available in the Malverna Public Library.

25
Say It In Translation

Because Marble College is situated several hundred miles from the nearest metropolitan area or any other sizable academic institution, an attitude of self-reliance has been consciously developed by the college in regard to building its library collections. Toward this end, in 1966 the two million dollar Heston Onelda Library (known as "Nellie" to Marble students) was completed with a total capacity for 700,000 volumes and seating space for 750 readers, including carrels, study tables, and large chairs which provide approximately 450 individual study units. The library's collections are currently placed at 280,000 volumes with eight to ten thousand volumes including bound periodicals being added each year. The Onelda Library, physically a graceful building, has an artistic browsing room, separate rooms for documents, maps, periodicals, and reserve books, and a handsome rare books room, in addition to the main stack and reference areas.

By accenting quality education and controlling the numerical growth of its student body, Marble has been able to successfully compete on the national level with institutions many times its size for outstanding students, despite the drawback of its insularity. Likewise, with an endowment in excess of 15 million dollars and its reputation for academic quality, Marble has had little trouble in attracting a consistently distinguished faculty and staff. Marble's president, Henry Mason Parkman, a humanistic scholar and a strong advocate of small, independent colleges, frequently speaks out against pessimistic academicians who predict the eventual disappearance of the small liberal arts college, by citing Marble's remarkable progress and vitality as prima facie evidence to the contrary. President Parkman makes the point that quantitative growth, important though it may be to American society in general, has little place at Marble, where the enrollment—1300 undergraduate and 250 graduate students—has remained relatively static for the past ten or so years. Judging from the bountiful response to Parkman's fund raising efforts in the past, Marble's alumni and friends must agree with him.

In March, the chairmanship of the political science department at Marble became vacant due to the death of the widely respected Professor Victor Reading, and Professor George Fulda was selected as Reading's successor. Fulda, a slight man whose appearance belies an aggressive, highly competitive personality, had risen to the rank of associate professor at a prominent eastern university when it became apparent that his chances for further advancement were unlikely. He therefore quickly accepted President Parkman's invitation to come to Marble, beginning in the fall semester.

It was not long after his arrival at Marble that Professor Fulda sought out the director of the college library, Frank Kelly, and complained that, while the library's collections in his own area of specialization—American government and diplomacy—were satisfactory, considering the severely limited size of the library operation, the materials available for research and study on contemporary affairs outside the United States— especially the important areas of Russian and Chinese affairs—were sorely inadequate, even for so small a library operation. Most certainly, Fulda told Kelly, the library should be subscribing to the major services which translate current foreign publications—invaluable sources for primary material. He pointed out that, with the exception of the *Current Digest of the Soviet Press, Soviet Law and Government*, and a few scattered issues of *Extracts from China Mainland Publications, t*he library had completely neglected these most important publications. Fulda further noted that many of the translation services which he had in mind— such as *Selections from China Mainland Magazines, Survey of China Mainland,* and the Central Intelligence Agency's *Daily Report: Foreign Radio Broadcasts*—were, to the best of his knowledge, available gratis from the U.S. State Department, although the most important of these services, the U.S. Government's *Joint Publications Research Service Publications*, was available only by subscription, if he remembered correctly.

After Professor Fulda had concluded his argumentation by remarking that many Communist countries, including China, do not publish annual national statistics, and that the only source of this type of information many times is the current press or radio broadcasts from each country, Frank Kelly promised that he would investigate the matter and decide which, if any, of these translation services the library could obtain, either gratis or by subscription. Kelly told Fulda that he doubted if the library could afford to expend much more than, perhaps, four or five hundred dollars on such material at the present time. The following year, of course, sufficient funds could be requested and appropriated—probably up to $5,000 if necessary. Fulda parted from Kelly, seemingly placated.

The librarian at Marble College is charged with overseeing the growth and development of the library's collections, and, with this end in mind, he controls and administers the book and periodicals budget. Ordinarily, Kelly has anywhere from $1,000 to $3,000 annually available for special purchases. It is from this fund that Kelly will draw if any translation sources are purchased this year.

■ After determining the full range of current translation sources available, indicate which ones you would recommend Onelda Library acquire this year, both as gifts, if possible, and on the subscription basis. What problems of acquisition may be involved, in addition to cost? Consider the validity of Professor Fulda's assertion that a library the size of Onelda should hold a wide range of English translation sources in the social sciences. In addition to services which translate current publications and broadcasts of the Soviet and Chinese press and radio, note similar sources for Latin America, Europe, Africa, and the Near East.

26
Teaching With Celluloid

When Helen Watson saw Sam Salvisberg come into the library, she instinctively began to look for something to do which would give her the appearance of being very busy. Miss Watson, associate librarian for audio-visual materials at Fort Hill High School, did not like Sam Salvisberg, but she tried not to show it. His cynical comments were annoying, but her job was to get along with *all* the teachers—and she worked hard to achieve this end.

True to form, Salvisberg, who taught history at Fort Hill, officiously browsed around the library, handling this and that, before acknowledging Miss Watson's presence. Much as she disliked him, and hoped that he would leave without speaking to her, Miss Watson regarded Salvisberg's aloofness as bad manners. Observing the common social amenities were particularly important to the successful functioning of Miss Watson's small, orderly world, and Salvisberg appeared to disdain all forms of politeness. When he finally did speak to Miss Watson—rudely interrupting her at her desk, busy at work—Salvisberg did not even say "good morning" or "hello," but only, "See you have some new records."

"Oh, Mr. Salvisberg—Sam. I didn't see you come in." Miss Watson smiled cheerfully, looking up from her desk. "Oh yes, we just processed some new ones. The Winston Churchill speeches may interest you."

"Saw them." Salvisberg made a face.

"You could send your world history class over. Perhaps a project?" Miss Watson continued to smile her unrelenting smile.

"Churchill was an old fool. An imperialist, out of step with his times. But a majestic fool, true. He could deliver a speech." Salivsberg was noted for his unorthodox views, and his willingness to let them be known. Last year—his first year at Fort Hill—he was the center of a minor flap when a student told his parents that Mr. Salvisberg had called Lincoln "a power-hungry dictator." Charles Tremont, the principal, had defended Salvisberg on this occasion, and, according to teachers' lounge gossip, Dr. Tremont had congratulated him for his intellectual candor in the classroom.

"India would have waited for years for her independence if that old buffoon had remained prime minister after the war. For once, bless them, the British acted with some sense."

"Nevertheless, Sam, many, many people regard Churchill as a *great* man."

"True. A serious cold war hangup and an imperialist mentality notwithstanding. Helen?"

"Yes?"

"It's April."

"April? Of course. It's been April for a week. Isn't it nice." Miss Watson glanced toward the spacious windows by her desk. "Why last night Mother and I sat on the porch and we could actually hear the peepers. Such sounds." Miss Watson continued to smile at Salvisberg, but she was suspicious. He was *not* a sentimentalist, she thought, and she doubted very much that April and peepers interested him in the least.

"You ought to get those peepers on a tape—make a record. Why the kids would flock—literally flock—in here, Helen. Think of it—Bo Peep and the Peepers. A new swingingest record. You could—"

"You're making fun of me, Sam."

"Hardly. Peepers are one of my favorite animals. Or bugs. Which are they, animals or bugs? Quick now."

"I don't exactly know—"

"Well, you *must* let me know. I won't sleep tonight. Honest. Now, let me tell you what April means to me."

"All right."

"The Spanish-American War, TR, Sun Yat-sen, the Russo-Japanese War. And toward the end of the month, Sarajevo, the Triple Alliance and Entente, U-boats, Ludendorff, Kerensky, Fourteen Points."

"Sounds like your world history class?"

"Right! You ought to go on a quiz show, Helen. So quick you are. Now, the *big* news is that, after a few weeks with the twenties and thirties, I move on to Weimar, Von Hindenburg, Danzig, Maginot, Dunkirk, Hitler. In short, I *will* get to war of the world number two for the first time in my brief teaching career. A genuine feat of pedagogical self-discipline, eh?"

"When I had world history in high school, the teacher never even got to the twentieth century."

"Which makes my feat all the more impressive. Now, some planning is required and you can help."

"What do you need?"

"How's things audio-and-visual-wise for World War Two?"

"Well, we don't have much here. No one has ever requested much in the past, but we do have one of the Edward R. Murrow 'Hear It Now' records with Hitler's voice. And there's probably several filmstrips, I think —I'll have to check. And, of course, I can get films from Drayton. Or direct if they don't have what you want."

Fort Hill High School, which accommodates grades nine through twelve, currently has a student body of 950. The new multimillion dollar high school building, attractively modernistic in design, was completed only last fall. A predominantly upper middle-class community of 27,000 population, Fort Hill is proudly "education conscious," and, as a result, the school system receives excellent financial support.

The high school library annually expends nearly $60 per pupil on books and other library materials, a statistic which Grace Gurney, the library coordinator for the system, quotes to every visiting school administrator or librarian. In addition to a book collection of some 19,000 volumes—including a large number of paperbacks—and 150 periodical subscriptions, the library is strong in audiovisual materials, which reflects Mrs. Gurney's emphasis on the library as an instructional materials center. At the present time, the library's rapidly growing audiovisual holdings include 475 phonograph records, approximately 400 filmstrips, a sizable number of tapes, and 53 16mm and 8mm films. It should be noted that most films used by teachers at Fort Hill are either rented directly or borrowed from the large film collection of the Drayton Public Library, a library serving a city of 900,000 and only twelve miles from Fort Hill. As might be expected, the library at Fort Hill has the latest audiovisual equipment available, including several mobile audiovisual carts for individual classroom use. Each cart provides a 16mm projector, a filmstrip projector, combination record player and tape recorder, an overhead projector, and slide projector.

"I don't want the usual canned films. I want to hit these kids—shake them up. Rome, Napoleon, even the American Civil War are too far removed from these kids. They're just names and meaningless facts. But World War Two I think I can make them feel." Salvisberg looked at Miss Watson, who smiled vaguely.

"You want special films?"

"Did you ever read Marc Bloch, the French historian? In the *Historian's Craft* he said something like, when the historian catches the scent of human flesh he's on the way to understanding the period he's studying."

"Sounds pretty gruesome to me."

"Now here's where I need your help. I'm going to give World War Two two weeks, probably June third to the fourteenth. What I want you to get me are five films—to show every other day—that will really get to these kids. I need one showing German concentration camps. The full horror—the whole bit. One on dropping the Bomb on Hiroshima. One on jungle warfare in the Pacific. One on the German invasion of Russia— something on Stalingrad would be best. And there's a Nazi propaganda film—*Kolberg*, I believe is the title—I'd like to show. Goebbels made it to bolster home front morale toward the end of the war. That's it."

"Most teachers have specific film titles in mind, Sam. And you should have requested these at the beginning of the year—or at least by January."

"My dear, I didn't know that I'd get up to World War Two. I don't have time to go through those catalogs and indexes. Besides, that's your job. At least that's what Gurney says at teachers' meeting."

"Well, I can't get films like that. I'm sorry, but we couldn't get them by June anyway. And films about concentration camps and Nazi propaganda are *not* considered educational films."

"Two months is plenty of time, even if you can't get them from Drayton. Come on, or I'll go around tonight and bump off every peeper in Fort Hill."

"I am sorry, Sam, but this request—well, next year you put in your requests at the proper time and we'll see what can be done."

"You're serious, aren't you? Damnit, you librarians are all alike. Afraid of your own shadows. Well—we'll see about this!" With this statement, Salvisberg wheeled and left the library. Miss Watson's smile faded completely.

The following afternoon, Grace Gurney stopped at Helen Watson's desk.

"Helen, I'm glad I caught you. What's all this fuss about with Sam

Salvisberg? He came into my office this morning, mad as a bull. I'm afraid he wasn't very complimentary to you or the library."

Miss Watson explained the situation as best she could, ending with a plaintive "if he had had his requests in sooner—"

"Now, Helen. I don't want you to worry about this, but I'm afraid we will have to try to help him, nasty as he is. He's threatened to go to Dr. Tremont, and if there's one thing I can't afford right now is an argument with Dr. Tremont. You know how he hangs on every word that boy says. He thinks Sam Salvisberg is an intellectual!"

"*I* think he's crude and horrible."

"I know, Helen, but you'll have to put that sentiment aside for now. Call him and find out exactly what he wants and try to get it for him. That boy. I just don't know—"

■ The Fort Hill High School library holds most of the major audio-visual guides, indexes, including *Educational Media Index,* and review sources. In addition, the library receives a number of film catalogs from major distributors. Which sources will be most useful to Miss Watson as she attempts to meet Salvisberg's film requests? What problems will she encounter with individual audiovisual reference sources? If she is not able to obtain *Kolberg,* the only specific title Salvisberg mentioned, what German war propaganda films could she substitute? Consider the state of bibliographic control of films and other audiovisual materials. Comment on Miss Watson's reaction to Salvisberg's request.

27
The Black Hole Of Calcutta

Weeding the vertical file was a job which Robert Berners, reference librarian at Gaylord College, usually put off until not another pamphlet, booklet, or odd bit of propaganda could be crammed into the bulging folders. And because the library's collected ephemera had once again reached that unhappy state of fullness, Berners girded himself for a morning of high-powered weeding. As he worked, Berners kept an eye on the reference desk, which was nearby.

He had just begun to tackle the D-G drawer when a student interrupted him.

"Hi. I'm back!" Berners' face registered a quizzical expression. "The guy you helped yesterday—remember?"

"Oh sure. I remembered your face but couldn't place it. The Black Hole of Calcutta, wasn't it?"

"That's right."

"Did you find enough information?"

"That's why I came over to see you today. I looked in that dictionary you showed me and sure enough it had just the stuff I was looking for. The number in the Hole, the number who died, etcetera."

"Glad it had what you wanted. Glad you're all set." Berners returned his attention to the glutted D-G drawer, signaling that, as far as he was concerned, the conversation was over.

"But I'm not really." The student persisted. "See, I looked at the other dictionary next to the first one—the one you showed me—to see if I could get more information. And it didn't agree."

Berners reluctantly pushed in the D-G drawer and leaned on the vertical file. "Didn't agree? About what?"

"Do you have a minute? Can I show you those two books? I would of yesterday, except I had a class."

"OK. You show me." Berners and the student walked across the room to the section of the reference collection dealing with history.

"Here's the one I looked at first—the one you showed me." The young man handed Berners Low and Pulling's *Dictionary of English History.* "Now just read this—under 'Black Hole of Calcutta'." Berners read:

> . . . the prisoners, 146 in number, were thrust into a narrow chamber, some twenty feet square. . . . The agonies endured during this terrible night were horrible beyond expression. The night was intensely hot, and as the torments of thirst and suffocation came upon them, the prisoners struggled with one another for a mouthful of fresh air at the windows. They insulted the guards to induce them to fire on them. The majority died in raving madness; and the few who survived owed their lives to the freer ventilation obtained by standing on the bodies of their dead or dying companions. Twenty-three ghastly survivors alone were dragged out the next morning. Mr. Holwell was so broken that he had to be carried before the Nawab, who manifest no compunction at the results of his infamous cruelty.

"Now, look at this one—here, on page forty." Berners saw that it was *A New Dictionary of British History*, edited by S.H. Steinberg. He quickly read the short entry:

> . . . 146 English prisoners are said to have been imprisoned in a small room of 18 by 15 feet, where 123 died of suffocation. The only source of this improbable story is John Holwell (1711-98), who had good reasons for glossing over the incompetence and cowardice of the British governor and council, of which he was a member.

"I don't see the problem. *Low and Pulling* say that the room was 18 by 15 feet while *Steinberg*—no, *Steinberg* says the room was—"

"That's not it. This one says that the story's improbable—not true. That one doesn't mention anything about not being true."

"Well, you're right about that." Berners shook his head. "In that case, I guess they don't agree, do they? But this is interesting. *Low* cites references—Macaulay and so on—whereas *Steinberg* doesn't give any. I'd be more inclined to trust *Low*, even though *Steinberg* is more recent. Why don't we look in the general encyclopedias—they're constantly revised and should clear up the discrepancy. They're right over here."

Rapidly checking both *Collier's Encyclopedia* and *Encyclopedia Americana,* Berners found that each agreed, substantially, with Low's *Dictionary of English History.* "Neither questions the truth of the incident. They don't agree on the number of people in the Hole or on the size, but the statistics aren't radically different. 146 as opposed to 143—"

"But look at this!" The student, who had had some difficulty finding *Encyclopaedia Britannica's* account, read part of the entry aloud: " 'The prisoners, numbering, according to the contemporary evidence, 146 persons (a modern estimate places the number as low as 64), were forced into the guardroom. . . .' What do you think of that! ?"

"But it doesn't substantiate what *Steinberg* says, though."

"This is *really* interesting. I might even be able to use it as a term paper topic for Mr. Goldsmith's course. Where could I find some more information, do you think?"

"Why not talk it over with Mr. Goldsmith first?"

"I can't because I have to show him that there's enough material on the subject before I have a conference. I was going to do something on the Boer War, but this sounds better—if there's anything on the subject."

"Let me get this straight. You want to do a paper on if the Black Hole incident was true, or on the statistical discrepancies, or on the subject in general?"

"I guess all three, in a way. The paper has to be on some detailed aspect of British foreign relations between 1688 and 1919—except we can't choose the American Revolution. It has to show how the event affected contemporary policy and all that stuff. See, with the Black Hole, I could work in Clive's conquest of India."

"What I'd do if I were you is check the card catalog for books on Indian and English history. Then check all volumes of *Historical Abstracts* for periodical articles. Maybe you'll be able to track down how true the incident was that way and at the same time get some good material for the general subject. I would guess that quite a bit's been written on the Black Hole. You might also want to look through the appropriate volume of the *Bibliography of British History*—I think it would be the Pargellis and Medley volume. And *Writings on British History*—don't forget that one. Got all that?"

"Hey, that's a big help. Thanks."

"And if you can't resolve those discrepancies, let me know. Maybe I can think of some other sources you could check. OK?"

"OK. I may be back. So long."

"So long." Berners returned to the fat D-G drawer of the vertical file, attacking it with renewed energy.

■ Gaylord College Library, which contains approximately 150,000 volumes and 740 current periodical subscriptions, serves some 1200 undergraduate students and a faculty of 95. Assuming that the library's collections in history and political science have been reasonably well chosen, will the student in this case be able to reconcile the conflicting information he found concerning the Black Hole of Calcutta? Will he be able to find enough material for a term paper on the Black Hole? How helpful will Berners' bibliographic suggestions be to the student?

28
Big Deal At Rich-Hood

After mechanically preparing her usual egg salad sandwich, Doris Bowman could not make up her mind if she preferred an orange or an apple for lunch. "The ole tick-tock's moving right around to twenty-two minutes before nine on this bee-u-u-tiful Friday morning, swingers." The announcer's words reminded her that she was late. Decisively, she switched off the radio, dropped the sandwich and an apple, less messy, into a frayed lunch bag, located her purse, and, after a final glance in the hall mirror, left the apartment.

Within seconds, Doris Bowman was part of the metropolitan traffic pattern, weaving her small sports car in and out of the automotive stream with greater daring than usual in an attempt to recoup the lost minutes. Once she entered the four lane highway complex which led directly to the Rich-Hood Electronics Corporation, she relaxed, knowing that by driving in the far left lane she could arrive at the library by nine o'clock. Before coming to Rich-Hood as research librarian three years ago, Miss Bowman had worked as a reference assistant in a large city library. Because the job had had little to offer her by way of authority or responsibility and was dull and routine, she had had little compunction about occasionally arriving late for work; but now, at Rich-Hood, she felt that her work was important, that she was part of an organization which was going somewhere and doing exciting things. She wheeled the small car into the Rich-Hood parking lot with a flourish at one minute before nine. Very gratifying.

Rich-Hood Electronics Corporation, a manufacturing firm which produces precision electronic equipment such as automatic door openers and marine instruments, employs a total of 280 persons, many of whom are scientists and engineers. A growing organization—output and profits have increased by more than 50 percent during the past five years—Rich-Hood owes its rapid development primarily to the efforts and energies of one man, Dwight Rich, president of the firm. A young, demanding, thorough, brilliant, aggressive businessman and organization manager who knows his products and his customers, Rich has been particularly successful in securing sizable contracts from the federal government. Very much an individualist in the nineteenth-century sense of that word, Rich does not fully subscribe to the values and organizational qualities of the "technostructure"—as Galbraith calls it—but he understands it and is willing to exploit it. Certainly, in the recent past Rich has not been reluctant to use unorthodox, albeit scrupulous, methods to get what he wants for the corporation.

Six years ago, Rich-Hood hired a librarian to establish a collection of materials to serve the firm's research needs. Today, this library contains nearly 3,500 books, over 200 periodical subscriptions, and more than 4,000 documents, including technical and annual reports, government publications, trade catalogs, patents, and reprints. In addition to Miss Bowman, who administers the library and holds the title of research librarian, two full-time clerical assistants are employed in the library.

After quickly eating her lunch at her desk, and getting egg salad on her dress, Miss Bowman continued working on a complicated literature search which she had begun earlier in the day. Working steadily, she had almost completed the project when she received a telephone call from Audrey Newcomb, Dwight Rich's secretary.

"Miss Bowman. I've just had a call from Mr. Rich—in Chicago. He asked me to contact you *right away*. He needs some information—about congressmen and a tax law. Mr. Rich said it's urgent. He wanted to speak to you personally but he said to tell you he couldn't because he was late for a meeting."

"I understand perfectly, Audrey. What is it he wants?"

"Do you have some paper handy? This is slightly complicated."

"I've got a pad. Now, what does Mr. Rich want?"

"I took this down in shorthand as Mr. Rich was speaking, so I'd get it right. He said, 'Ask Miss Bowman to find out which congressmen from New York state voted for and against the—the foreign subsidiary provision—of the law which—amended the, er, the Internal Revenue Law—of 1954.' He said it was passed in 1961 or 1962—sometime in Kennedy's term. He said you'd know about it. It's the one he was so mad about because of his expense account."

"I don't remember that—must have been before my time. But that shouldn't be too difficult, Audrey. I'll stop by the Mishawum Public tonight on the way home."

"Oh, but that's not all, Miss Bowman. He also wants to know, 'If any New York congressmen introduced amendments dealing with the foreign subsidiary provision and how each senator and representative voted on —voted on those amendments, if there were any.' "

"Each *New York* senator and representative?"

"That's right—each one from New York. Ready for the next part?"

"Shoot."

"Next he wants to know, 'If any New York legislators who are still in congress spoke for or against the—the foreign subsidiary provision, when it was being—being debated in congress. And make copies of their remarks.' Got that?"

"Think so. Who, still in congress, spoke on the provision. Copy their remarks."

"Next he—"

"Look, Audrey, why don't I come over to your office? Sarah's here and I can get away."

"Well—there isn't too much more to go—just two more parts—."

"All right, go ahead." Miss Bowman shifted the telephone to her other ear.

"Next he wants to know, 'If any New York legislators who are—' Sorry —I just gave you that part. The next is, 'Were any—congressional hearings held on this section of the bill when it was being considered—and did any New York industrialists testify before—before the investigating committee?' "

"Any hearings? Anyone testify? Got that. What else?"

"The last thing is, 'Ask Miss Bowman to get a copy of the provision of the law dealing with subsidiaries of United States corporations in foreign countries—' "

"Sorry to interrupt, Audrey, but is that the same as the foreign subsidiary provision of this 1961 law? The one we've been talking about?"

"I guess so. It's the only one he's interested in. I suppose he just wants a copy. You know Mr. Rich—likes everything neat and organized."

"OK. Copy the provision. That's it?"

"That's all Mr. Rich gave me to tell you. He just said, 'Ask Miss Bowman to have this information on my desk tomorrow at noon.' "

"By tomorrow at *noon!*"

"Mr. Rich said it's very urgent. He's coming back from Chicago Saturday—tomorrow morning. He's due in on Eastern flight forty-seven at 10:18."

"Well, Audrey, wish me luck. It's been sometime since I've dug around in the *Congressional Record.*"

■ The solution to this case involves finding the information which Mr. Rich has requested and presenting it in such a manner that he can easily pinpoint textual material, facts, and quotations. Before undertaking the search, consider the most efficient way in which the information may be secured by carefully examining such reference tools as the *Congressional Record, Digest of Public General Bills, C.Q. Almanac and C.Q. Weekly Report, Congressional Digest,* Commerce Clearing House's *Congressional Index, United States Code,* and *The Statutes at Large of the United States.* Discuss the problems encountered while searching for the requested information and evaluate the various reference tools used.

29
Through The One-Way Mirror

It was early September, and the languid easiness which settled over the Sefton University campus between the end of summer school and the beginning of the fall semester had begun to give way to that happy tension created by students and faculty returning to the groves after weeks or months of music festivals, sunny beaches, cabins in Vermont, trips through the West or to Mexico or Europe, reading or writing books, mowing lawns, or working for state highway departments. Many trunks and boxes were being unloaded and unpacked in the dormitories; friendships, casual relationships, and personal enmities were being renewed, rescued, talked about, or formed; apartments in Hazelmere, very much a University Town, were becoming scarce, and some students were beginning to feel panicky about their housing prospects; the student union was suddenly busy and noisy again.

Paul Bonair, a young assistant professor of sociology in the College of Social Science at Sefton, was among the early returnees. Last week, he and his wife and two daughters drove to Hazelmere from Seattle, where they had spent a leisurely month visiting relatives and old friends. Dr. Bonair had insisted upon returning at least three weeks before classes began, so he could do some last minute work on his "Collective Behavior" course. "I've only taught it once, Janet," he told his wife, "and there's a lot of rough edges that need work." At this moment, Dr. Bonair is on his way to the university library to attend to several small matters. His old Edsel, which had made the trip to Seattle and back without a major breakdown, did not sound very healthy, but Bonair put this down to engine exhaustion and dismissed the pinging sounds from his mind.

Sefton University, with a total enrollment of over 14,000 students, including 4,500 engaged in graduate study, is composed of eight colleges,

138

which function as a closely joined confederation under the general direction of the university president. The university also supports several research bureaus, including the influential Gilbert Social and Political Research Center. The College of Social Science, where Dr. Bonair teaches, is one of the largest colleges at Sefton in terms of numbers of students and faculty. Subdivided into the departments of anthropology, economics, geography, police science and public safety, political science, psychology, social work, sociology, and urban planning, the College of Social Science offers a wide range of programs for both graduate and undergraduate students.

Dr. Bonair guided the pinging Edsel into the parking lot adjacent to the library. Through force of habit, he locked the car, though he doubted anyone would want to steal it. Once in the library, he returned several books to the circulation desk, and then inquired if Bill Wardman was in the library office.

"I believe Mr. Wardman is still on vacation, Professor Bonair. But Mr. Mann is in."

"Is he the new social science bibliographer?"

"I don't really know how long he's been here—I only started working this summer, and he was here when I came."

"Where's his office? I want to see someone about some books for a course I'm teaching."

"Just go to the social science library office, and his office is off to the right. One of the girls in the office will show you where it is."

The Sefton University Library is organized on a broad divisional plan. The three divisional libraries—humanities, social science, and education and science—each employ several subject specialists, called bibliographers, who are primarily responsible for selection of current and retrospective materials. Bibliographers usually hold advanced degrees in a subject field as well as professional library training.

Dr. Bonair entered the large library office, approached a pretty young girl who was typing, identified himself, and asked for Mr. Mann.

"That's his office over there, but I don't think he's in right now. Is it important? I can try to get him—."

"No—I just want to be sure that these books," Bonair produced a list, "will be ready by the twenty-seventh."

"Have you received notification cards on them?"

"Only for two. That's what bothers me. I need all of them for the first several weeks of the semester. Usually Bill Wardman takes care of this sort of thing for me. Who else can I see?"

"Well—Mr. Wardman's on vacation, but he will be back on Monday and then you—" Just then, John Mann walked into the office. "Oh, here's Mr. Mann now. Mr. Mann? He'll be able to help you. Excuse me. Oh Mr. Mann?"

"Yes, Anne?"

"This is Dr. Bonair from the sociology department. He's here about some books for one of his courses."

"Jack Mann—how do you do. I've seen your name on order cards, but never had the pleasure."

"Paul Bonair. You're working with Bill Wardman as a social science bibliographer?"

"That's right. I came to Sefton last February." John Mann, thirty years old, has a master's degree in sociology and is currently attending a nearby library school where he has completed five courses toward a professional qualification. "You have a question about some books? Let's go into my office." After getting seated in Mann's cramped little office, Bonair explained the purpose of his trip to the library.

"I'm particularly concerned about Handy and Kurtz's *Current Appraisal of the Behavioral Sciences.* I need at least five copies for the 'Collective Behavior' course at the beginning of the semester. I'd make it a required purchase, but I only use it for about two weeks."

"I know the book—it's a good one."

"For my purposes, it's almost perfect. "Collective Behavior" is basically an undergraduate course, and at the very outset I emphasize the interdisciplinary nature of the social and behavioral sciences as applied to collective behavior—and Handy and Kurtz is about the best book available to introduce interdisciplinary relationships."

"I'll be glad to check on that one for you. And if you leave your list, I'll check on the others, too."

"I'd appreciate whatever you can do. This is only the second time I've taught the course, and I'm making a few minor changes."

"Sounds like an interesting course to teach."

"It is. It's a welcome change, too, from 'Introduction to Sociology.'"

"I had 'Behavior of Groups'—probably the same course."

"Probably. Where did you do your work?"

"Midland State."

"You probably had Miles Orne—he's been at Midland for some years, I believe."

"Oh, sure. Dr. Orne was there. In fact, I had a seminar on social and behavioral attitudes with him. Now there's a teacher who can really stimulate."

"I have a real respect for Orne. He's done some significant work. But this latest study—the one on habits of cheaters—is a bit hard to take, don't you think?"

"I participated in some of Dr. Orne's experiments—I don't know what you mean? 'Hard to take?'"

"It's the business of ethics that bothers me. Having selected students induce others to cheat and then observing their reactions through one-way glass and listening devices—that strikes me as professionally unethical."

"Dr. Orne—and I would agree—believes that sociologists—any social scientist—must be value-free. Certainly, if the social sciences are to be scientific, this must be the case. Beliefs and feelings—and ethical codes—have no place in science. Investigators can't allow the prevailing morality to influence their collection and evaluation of data. Their findings are *per se* non-ethical."

"That's a rather naive approach, isn't it, Mr. Mann?"

"I don't think so. It's an established methodological fact that if the subject of an empirical investigation knows he's being observed he frequently reacts differently than he would if he didn't know it. You're familiar certainly with the green light experiments?—where those who talked least when they didn't know they were being observed, talked most when experimenters later revealed themselves."

"I don't recall that specific experiment, and I wouldn't dispute the results. That's not the point. I'm saying that no social scientist can achieve the 'ethical neutrality' Weber talked about. Durkheim tried and failed, although *theoretically* his position as stated in the *Rules of Sociological Method* is unassailable. In fact, I believe the social scientist *should* have an ethical or moral or whatever-you-want-to-call-it position so he can make the necessary value judgments about what's important and what isn't. Otherwise, he'll simply collect random data on random subjects. And if the social scientist does accept the prevailing social ethic, he must work within that ethical framework. *And,* if he does that, then one-way glass is—"

"One-way *mirrors.*"

"One-way mirrors then—are out."

"Well, Dr. Bonair, I would just say that if people *do* tend to act differently when they're observed openly, and you *don't* think the investigator has the right to use corrective methodology, how in the world can social science ever hope to collect enough accurate data to eventually predict human behavior?"

"Methodology will simply have to take this variance into account—just as opinion pollers do. Much more important, it seems to me, is the need for social scientists to stop hiding behind one-way glass and get out into the community—into the political structure. Too often basic research simply becomes a neurotic escape from decision making."

"But you don't seem to understand—it's not the scientist's job to make political decisions, or be a reformer. The chemist or the physicist can't be concerned if his discoveries are used to destroy or build. His obligation is to science. Dr. Orne always said that to politicize science was to kill its objectivity—and thus science itself. Look at the Russian government's attitude toward any psychological conclusions which differ from Pavlov's behaviorism. Scientists belong in the laboratory where they can remain value-free."

"Then we simply disagree, Mr. Mann. You want the social scientist to be a value-free empiricist, and I want him to be a social engineer. Look! —all social scientists are guided by the value system into which they were born and operate. They're human, bound to their backgrounds, their own experiences and biases, their goals. Why is American sociology predominantly empirical while European is theoretical? Simply because Americans are pragmatic and happen to have a great many pressing social problems, like race relations, which need solved. That's all."

"I would agree when you say that the social scientist can't completely escape his biases and so forth, but you're not allowing for the scientific method as a check on these human factors. Since observation by qualified observers under controlled conditions is an integral part of this procedure, the investigator *can* overcome his biases and choose the best conditions. That's why I defend Dr. Orne. He's a pure scientist using the most objective method to gather his data. You *do* remember what Ogburn said in *Science and Civilization*, don't you?"

"Yes—beware the theory-builders, the system-builders, for they steal the glory from the hardworking empiricists. Dear old Ogburn. Empirical as American sociology is, it was never empirical enough. Nevertheless, Ogburn and Orne to the contrary, I believe that social scientists are

bound to their humanity—their humanness. And this necessitates working within a particular value system. If unethical, deceitful methods of
gathering data are used, the society won't stand for it. My hunch is that
answers to most social problems such as cheating won't come from the
kind of data Orne is collecting, anyway. Rather, I suspect that asocial
and antisocial behavior are a result of the moral climate. Perhaps the
scientist's first duty is to set an honest example."

"But what you're forgetting, Dr. Bonair, is—"

"What I'm forgetting, Mr. Mann, is that I'm supposed to meet my wife
at Braemore's in five minutes. I really have to go."

"Well, I'm glad I finally got to meet you. This talk was fun—maybe
when Bill gets back we could all get together sometime and continue
this."

"Sounds like a good idea. You won't forget about checking on those
books, will you?"

"No, I'll give you a ring tomorrow."

■ Evaluate the issues raised by the discussion between Bonair and
Mann. Which arguments do you support? Disagree with? How do social
scientists currently view the question of professional ethics? "Ethical
neutrality"? The value of basic versus applied research?

30
Waiting For The Computer

"Good morning, Mr. Pike. How are you today?"

"Fine, thanks. Yourself?"

"Just fine and dandy. It's such a lovely day out. Will you have a chair? Mr. Hathaway will be with you in just a minute."

Morgan Pike sat down and began searching his pockets for a cigarette. Eventually, he found a fresh pack, opened it, and after borrowing a match from Hathaway's secretary, lit a cigarette, taking a deep pull and exhaling the smoke slowly. A youngish man who wears a boyish crewcut, Pike is one of seven subject specialists on the reference staff at Abbotsford State University Library. With a master's degree in both education and library science, Pike came to Abbotsford as a specialist in education directly after completing his graduate work in librarianship. Sometime in the future, he plans to study for a doctorate in education.

Pike was leafing through a current issue of the *New Yorker*, looking at the cartoons, when Charles Hathaway appeared in the outer office. Hathaway, coordinator of reference and research services at Abbotsford, greeted Pike and ushered him into his office.

"Sit down. Over here."

"Thank you."

"How's everything, Mr. Pike? You've been with us—what?—for about a year?"

"That's right. Eleven months now."

"Enjoying it?"

"Oh very much."

"Cigarette?"

"Thanks."

"Now, Mr. Pike, what's on your mind?"

144

"Sorry. Do you happen to have a match?" Hathaway produced a lighter.

Pike took a short puff on his cigarette. "I made this appointment with you, Mr. Hathaway, to get your opinion on a project I'm interested in for the School of Education." When Hathaway made no move to respond to this statement, Pike continued. "Getting directly to the point, I think it would be a good idea to try getting out some kind of abstract of the education literature we receive in the library. Certainly, UNESCO with *Education Abstracts* hasn't been as successful in education as in other areas of the social sciences." Hathaway nodded his concurrence. "And ERIC—useful as it is—has its limitations. Our people don't like microfiche, and it's not selective enough."

"I haven't had occasion to use ERIC documents extensively, but I do know that some little time is spent on screening the material. As for microfiche, it's simply a matter of getting used to the format."

"You certainly have a point, but I don't think many of our faculty or students would agree. And that's basically why I've been thinking in terms of a local publication—one which would abstract—very concisely, of course—the most important articles, books, government publications, yearbooks, and so on that we receive in the library. Initially, at least, I'd limit the service to, say, forty or fifty core journals and the most basic books and other publications. Until we see how it goes, it could be a mimeographed affair and then, if it proved worthwhile, perhaps we could negotiate with the University press to run it off and advertise for subscriptions. This would not only be good publicity for the University and the library, but it would probably be a very welcome bibliographic tool for other college reference departments—and large public libraries. We *might* even be able to get a grant and expand its scope."

"How frequently would you plan to bring this abstract out?"

"Oh, probably monthly. We could start monthly and see how it goes. Any less frequently would limit its usefulness, I think. It's a matter of time-lag."

"Doesn't *Education Index* already do this job—essentially? Better, I'd say, than a homemade effort possibly could. Along with ERIC, of course."

"Well—the problem with *Education Index* is that it doesn't index books or much foreign periodical literature. And, two, it doesn't selectively index. And, three, it doesn't, naturally, abstract what it covers. And, of course, it doesn't index exactly what we get here. An abstracting service produced here at the library would selectively abstract the publications *we* receive, and that's really what we need at this point."

"You would do the selecting, I gather?"

"Yes. I'm familiar enough with the name authors in the field—the important authors. After all, I have a master's in ed."

"How much time would this involve? Just in round figures."

"Oh, I don't know—maybe fifteen hours a week. And I have two graduate students for ten hours a week and I figure they could get involved in some of the mechanics of the operation. Actually, the whole process wouldn't involve anything I don't do already. The only thing I don't do now is write the abstracts and have them printed for circulation. I figure it's part of my job to be on top of the literature in my field, and I constantly scan the publications we receive. Sometimes I call or drop a note to a professor who's interested in something I don't think he'd see otherwise. The faculty interest file is really helpful in this respect—and the nice thing is it's up-to-date."

"How many items would you abstract each month?"

"That's hard to tell. It would depend on the literature in a given month. But I'd say about—let's see—maybe fifty or sixty entries. At least in the beginning." Pike paused and looked at Hathaway, who was lighting another cigarette.

"Another cigarette?" Pike accepted Hathaway's cigarette. "Frankly, Mr. Pike, I don't think anyone would use a source such as the one you're proposing."

Pike's face fell a bit, looking like an astronaut who had just been told that he wasn't fit for the moon flight. Hathaway offered his lighter. "Thanks. Well, I think the faculty in the School of Education would go for it. I was talking to Professor Montelle the other day and I broached this idea—very circumspectly—and he seemed to think an abstracting service like this would be very useful to him and the School. Bibliographic control being what it is in education—in all the social sciences for that matter."

Abbotsford State University is the largest publicly supported institution of higher education in one of the rapidly developing southwestern states. The University's reputation was severely damaged several years ago when the state's Department of Education was obliged to investigate charges that Abbotsford's president, Dr. Howard Burr, had suppressed academic freedom, interfered with the freedom traditionally enjoyed by the undergraduate newspaper, and harassed certain faculty members who had openly criticized his administration of the University by deny-ing them promotions and tenure. Dr. Burr responded to these accusations by publicly charging the faculty and general student body with disloyalty, disrespect, and subversive conduct. However, despite the acrimonious charges and counter-charges, only a few of the dissident teachers actually resigned after the lengthy investigation failed to reach definite conclu-sions. Apparently, Dr. Burr made several concessions privately, and the campus of 10,500 graduate and undergraduate students returned to its customary placidity, at least on the surface.

The University library, which has a collection totaling 700,000 volumes, is organized as a consolidated unit, the divisional plan having been con-sidered and rejected when the new main library building was con-structed in 1959. The attempt has been to staff the reference department with subject specialists and, generally speaking, the effort has been suc-cessful. The specialists, in addition to providing reference assistance to students and faculty, are actively engaged in book selection, both current and retrospective. Specifically, Pike's duties include responsibility for overseeing the growth of the education collection, which usually adds be-tween 2,000 and 2,500 individual publications annually and subscribes to some 350 periodicals.

Hathaway adjusted his glasses. "Professors don't use abstracts and indexes—and all the other array of bibliographical utensils that have been developed. Most of their so-called 'searching'—I think you'd agree, Mr. Pike—is done through informal channels—through verbal exchange. One man tells the other about this or that important article or book or piece of ongoing research."

"That's true—to an extent."

"But when they're asked how to improve bibliographical control, they *always,* to a man, say 'more abstracts, more indexes, more bibliographies.' The point is that scholars *don't like* to use bibliographical tools. They're not lazy, just indifferent. And what's more, few of them even know the existing tools in their own field. For example, when I was doing univer-sity reference work—not that many years ago, either—I constantly ran into historians who had *never* heard of *Historical Abstracts,* economists who didn't know about *Economic Abstracts.*"

"But, Mr. Hathaway. Wouldn't they look at and use a highly selective service—which is really what the abstract I'm proposing would be? It would be sort of a summary sheet. And, it seems to me that students in the field could make good use of it, too. There's something like 260 or 270 graduate students in education here alone—"

"It's my thought that information retrieval—locating relevant material on some subject—which is what we're talking about—is more a matter of verbal exchange than of abstracting and indexing. The kind of service you're suggesting won't help scholars because they wouldn't use it. And even if you could somehow overcome their natural reluctance to use a tool—an abstract—like this, they wouldn't trust you—a librarian—to select the most important, the most significant material. As far as students are concerned, they are the ones who need a comprehensive bibliographical service. Part of their education is to find the relevant material out of the whole corpus. A graduate student, for example, who begins a thesis on, say, some aspect of secondary education in Brazil doesn't need *selective* tools—he must find, first, everything which has been written on the subject, then read it—or skim it—and make evaluations."

"I'm not—"

"The real breakthrough, Mr. Pike, in bibliographical control for social science literature will be realized when computerized information storage and retrieval is a commonplace in libraries. Then we can begin to think in terms of something approaching comprehensive control of the literature. *Index Medicus* is a good example of how the social sciences must begin to move—"

"But Mr. Hathaway. Until computers *become* commonplace, isn't some sort of *selective* control required? Doesn't the great increase of publication—in all fields and sub-fields—require selectivity? I recall reading somewhere that the quantity of publications is doubling—tripling—something like that—every ten years or so. The American Psychological Association's study of information exchange indicated that only a very small number of psychologists have *time* to read even *half* the articles which appear in the most important psych journals. I'm not even convinced that computers are necessary for this kind of sorting out of the literature."

"I follow your point. I'm familiar with the APA's study and I believe you have stated *one* of the many conclusions of that study. However, my point is that another abstracting publication won't help matters. It would be a waste of your time—and the library's time. Time you could easily afford to put into selection or helping students." Hathaway looked at his watch. "I'm afraid I'm going to have to break up this interesting conversation, Mr. Pike. I hope you're not too disappointed by my negative reactions to your idea."

"Well, I appreciate your taking so much time to talk this over with me—."

"I like your enthusiasm, Mr. Pike. But don't get carried away. Your idea has merit and the right motive, but the realities are such that it wouldn't make much of a contribution—at least at this time. Let's wait for the computer, what do you say?"

■ Being aware that existing resources should be fully investigated and exploited before the compilation of any kind of bibliography is undertaken, how would you evaluate Pike's proposal for an abstracting service in the field of education? Based on reading you have done dealing with bibliographic issues and problems, analyze the positions taken by Pike and Hathaway in their discussion of Pike's proposal. Do you believe, for example, that Hathaway is correct in discouraging Pike's abstracting project? Would professors and researchers in the field of education at Abbotsford, and elsewhere, be reluctant to use a selective tool compiled by a librarian with Pike's qualifications? Is it true, as Hathaway claims, that persons actively engaged in research do not use the existing bibliographic tools? Is Hathaway's faith in the promise of the computer's application to information storage and retrieval realistic? Comment on Hathaway's suggestion that *Index Medicus* should serve as an example for the bibliographic future of the social sciences.

Five Sample Student Analyses of Case Thirty

The five student analyses which follow are included to give the reader some sense of the case method in action, and to support several generalizations about the method expressed in the *Preface*. Teachers and students using this collection as a text should understand that *none of these analyses is intended as a prototype*. Each analysis simply illustrates how one individual student at a given time and place—in this instance, the fall 1967 semester at Simmons—elected to handle case thirty.

And it should become apparent after examining these five examples that individual student analyses of the same case can and frequently do differ —sometimes markedly—in their identification and treatment of issues, amount and type of documentation, organization of material, and style and format of presentation. For example, compare Virginia Clark's assessment of Pike's basic idea—a "modest proposal [which] merely extends the normal function of the librarian"—with Paul Brawley's—the result would be "a bibliographic disgrace." Or compare Edith Hathaway's straightforward style with C. M. Keen's or Joan Shepardson's more novel effort. This freedom of approach is an integral part of the case methodology.

But no matter how the student views the problems in a case study or presents his analysis, he must offer convincing arguments for his conclusions. Has Miss Clark, for example, constructed an airtight case for her position on Pike's proposed venture into bibliography? If so, what is to be said about Mr. Brawley's position? or Mrs. Shepardson's? What is important here—from the educational standpoint—is not so much the conclusions themselves but the thought processes which led to those conclusions.

SAMPLE ANALYSIS / I
By Edith Hathaway

The case of Pike vs. Hathaway opens up a wealth of problems and itchy issues to confront any fighting student of library science. In fact, one begins to feel like a lawyer searching around for the latest information as well as the most poignant and relevant case histories dealing with bibliographic problems, the science of indexing and abstracting, the relative merits of the *Education Index,* ERIC, and *Index Medicus,* the extent to which researchers use the available bibliographic tools, and the current experiments in computerized abstracting services. . . . But here, alas, are one fighter's findings.

To begin with, Hathaway is right to discourage Pike's proposed abstracting project. In spite of Pike's claim that he devotes most of his time already toward scanning the education literature received by the Abbotsford State University Library, it would not be practical for him to tackle such a large venture alone. This point of view is defended by M.B. Line in his article on the subject in the July, 1966 issue of *Aslib Proceedings.*

> Even if university libraries could index their periodicals, they should not attempt to, because the duplication of effort would be colossal. What is needed is a central computer file, whether with complete coverage or divided by broad subject group like MEDLARS, which could be searched for the answers to individual queries.[1]

Such a system would consequently necessitate regularly issued subject indexes by the individual libraries, indicating their own holdings, and printed out from a central computer tape, along with a tape recording the periodicals held by each library.

When Pike estimates it will take him from ten to fifteen hours a week to put out the proposed abstracting journal, it is difficult to believe he has thought out all the procedures involved. For he will have to consider the same items that must be considered in the effective use of any information retrieval system, namely: 1) the subject vs. descriptive approach; 2) how to restrict the language; 3) the acquisition policy; 4) the format

---

[1] M. B. Line, "University Libraries and the Information Needs of the Researcher: a Provider's View," *Aslib Proceedings,* XVIII (July, 1966), p. 183.

of the document; 5) the filing rules; 6) the search strategy (for example, key-word-in-context; hundreds of methods to choose from); 7) the format of the output; and 8) the user's needs.

Taking the last item alone, it is very unlikely that working by himself Pike will be able to adequately anticipate his user's needs. In fact, according to Paul Wasserman, in his book *The Librarian and the Machine,* it is even unlikely that computerized processes such as the SDI (Selective Dissemination of Information) will be able to do this successfully in academic libraries in the near future due to the enormous variety in the potential range of interest. To explain further, the first part of the SDI process involves the identification of the particular topics which comprise the interest profile of those individuals to be served by the system. And for Pike, this would require him to analyze the subject needs of his clients in a continuous and penetrating way. To date, there have been comparatively few university libraries to develop the SDI program.

But what about Pike and Hathaway's comments on *Education Index* and ERIC? Can they be justified? . . . In his *Sources of Information in Social Sciences,* Carl White tells us that *Education Index* is "the basic source for keeping abreast of the literature, . . . and excellent as a subject heading list."[2] Coming from Carl White, this makes *Education Index* sound thoroughly respectable. However, Pike is still right in saying it doesn't index books or much foreign periodical literature, that it doesn't index selectively, and that it doesn't do any abstracting. To compensate for some of these failings there is ERIC, which spelled out is the Educational Research Information Center. Operating as a branch of the U. S. Office of Education, ERIC acquires, abstracts, indexes, stores, retrieves, and disseminates nationally the most significant and timely educational research and research-related documents. It does not normally include reports that are more than five years old or copyrighted material, unless the copyright owners will sign an agreement to let copies be reproduced by ERIC for sale. In fact, it would seem that Hathaway and Pike are overlooking some important features of ERIC, especially in regard to the availability of items indexed and abstracted in ERIC's catalog. ERIC has a contract with the micro-photo firm Bell & Howell, Cleveland, Ohio to produce in the form of microfiche or hard copy any of the items in the catalog. And though this service does focus rather exclusively on

---

[2] Carl H. White, *Sources of Information in the Social Sciences* (Totowa, New Jersey: Bedminster Press, 1964), p. 339.

research materials, it is at least performing a function that *Education Index* does not to any extent. Another basic difference between ERIC and most other national information systems is that it is decentralized, there being thirteen clearing houses at the present time to cover thirteen different topics in education.

When Pike speaks in opposition to the usability of microfiche he is not being very reasonable. First of all, microfiche does not require any special filing equipment, just a 'microfiche reader,' which enlarges their images back to normal page size, is noiseless, compact, and requires no special skills to operate. The reader's cost is usually about $150. In addition, the microfiche form is much less expensive than the hard copy, as well as having the advantage of conserving on space. So surely, given the relative assets of ERIC and *Education Index* together, Pike could not hope to do anywhere near the same job with a homemade effort.

Now we come to the question of whether professors and researchers in the field of education at Abbotsford, and elsewhere, would actually make substantial use of an abstracting service such as the one Pike proposes. Pike says he spoke to one of the professors about it, and that this professor claimed it would be very useful to him and to the School. But both Pike and Hathaway refer to the findings of the APA (American Psychological Association) study, and regardless of the pleas Pike makes as to the usefulness of a "summary sheet" to both students and professors, the facts yielded from the APA study are a strong argument against Pike's project. Furthermore, an examination of the article in which the first results of the APA study were given reveal that Pike is citing correct information, but that he is woefully misinterpreting it, whether to suit his own purposes or not. Here is what is said on one crucial point.

> The data suggest that about half the articles in 'core' journals will be immediately read in the specialized sense of the word, by one percent or less of a random sample of psychologists, and no research report is likely to be read by more than seven percent.[3]

Although we have no similar statistics from a study of scholars and reseachers in education, we can reasonably assume that the same situation exists in this field, especially since education has normally involved even

---

[3] William D. Garvey and Belver C. Griffith, "Scientific Information Exchange in Psychology," *Science,* CXLVI (December 25, 1964), p. 1658.

less exchange of scientific data than psychology. Bearing this in mind, we can certainly support Hathaway's statement that "another abstracting publication won't help matters." The article also reinforces Hathaway's remarks that scholars are more apt to use verbal exchange than abstracting and indexing. The authors state that there are numerous elements in the general communication system of psychologists, foremost among which are preprint exchange, conventions, and private publications. But, significantly, their own journals are not at all the key medium of information exchange.

An inquiry similar to that of the APA was undertaken at the State University of Ghent in 1965, in which these two questions were explored: 1) "What exactly is the literature research method generally adopted by the social science research worker, and 2) what does he think about the efficiency of a documentalist's assistance?"[4] The persons interviewed were twenty colleagues of the authors, all of whom had at one time or another been engaged in social science research at the State University of Ghent, Department of the Faculty of Law and the School for Economics.

It was found that the beginning research worker far preferred to carry out his research independently, though he was willing to listen to the literature tips of subject specialists. As to the more experienced worker, it was found that he was more likely to avoid the vast array of bibliographic lists at the outset, and rely on his own experience and knowledge of documentation to take him to direct acquisition. His actions would thus be based on information from both specialized publishers and outstanding journals in the particular field. To further support the stand taken here that persons actively engaged in research use the existing bibliographical tools relatively little, we have this statement from the men of Ghent.

> . . . One may not conclude that the experienced research worker deliberately neglects the value of bibliographical tools. But as far as their practical use is concerned, he only consults them occasionally to fill in his knowledge of the documentation available in his nearest surroundings.[5]

Regarding abstracting services in particular, we have the following state-

---

[4] L. Uytterschaut, "Literature Searching Methods in Social Science Research: a Pilot Inquiry," *The American Behavioral Scientist*, IX (May, 1966), p. 14.
[5] *Ibid.*, p. 25.

ment as a summary of the responses to the question concerning what kinds of literature and/or other sources are consulted in keeping abreast of current findings.

Primary attention is given to leading journals and their sections on book reviews. In the second instance, lists of acquisitions of libraries and catalogues of book publishers are used. Then occasionally, different kinds of contacts between specialists, and, finally, abstracting journals, trend reports, and conference proceedings.[6]

This is a significant discovery about the amount of practical use given abstracting journals by scholars and researchers in the social sciences. It is quite a different story for the natural sciences, which, for a variety of reasons have very actively used abstracting journals.

In response to the second question cited, the men of Ghent found that research experience or field experience did not seem to be a determining factor in the usefulness of a documentalist's assistance. In light of this, we might reasonably conclude that Pike's background as a library school-trained-subject specialist would not greatly affect the willingness of professors and researchers in the field of education to use the selective tool he has proposed. The larger questions are, of course, whether these professors and researchers would use the tools substantially at all, and whether it is at all practical for Pike to attempt it alone.

Since the answers to both of these questions have been determined to the negative, what can we say of a more positive nature about the probability of computerized abstracting services becoming commonplace in libraries in the near future? N. W. Wood, in his article in *Aslib Proceedings* of June, 1966 doubts very much that we shall see the time when computers and retrieval machines will deal solely with micro-reductions of original articles. Using computers to abstract from the originals has been done experimentally, as with ERIC and *Index Medicus,* but the process involves the computer scanning the article so as to make word and phrase associations, which unfortunately combine to form a rather unsubstantial abstract, and may often emphasize irrelevant material or incorrect associations. There are a great many problems remaining to be solved, then, and many of them revolve around the fact that little has been done in linguistic data processing, and certainly nothing to approach the sophistication of the numeric languages such as FOR-

---

[6] *Op. cit.*

TRAN and ALGOL. Still, there is good reason to suppose that if librarians put on the pressure, the computer industry would soon realize what increasingly profitable business could be derived from the automatic processing of linguistic information.

Speaking of sophisticated numeric languages, one should note the growing effectiveness of MEDLARS, the digital computer system which, since January, 1964, has printed *Index Medicus*. Hathaway is right when he suggests that this index should serve as an example for the bibliographic future of the social sciences, and for the following reasons. Though not alone in being computer-produced (ERIC, *Chem. Abstracts, Psych. Abstracts,* and Alfred de Grazia's *Universal Reference System*), *Index Medicus* can be praised for its extent of foreign coverage; the fact that all titles are in English, or translated into English with titles in original language also given; its cumulated subject and author indexes; its annual list of subject headings (6,500 subject headings in the January, 1966 issue); its arrangement with the National Library of Medicine, stating its Interlibrary Loan Policy, its publications, and its literature searches; and its interdisciplinary coverage. Regarding the last point, there is this pertinent statement from Medical Library Association Bulletin.

> Recent expansions in indexing policy have involved greater coverage of such fields as biology, chemistry, physics, veterinary medicine, pharmacy, dentistry, and the behavioral sciences.[7]

And of course, if Alfred de Grazia has his way, the social sciences will also witness a virtual renaissance in the interdisciplinary quality of their bibliographies and indexes.

Other problems which must be met involve including in the abstracts and the journals a greater number of the current articles being written in a given field, and increasing the speed between the time an article is submitted, published, and abstracted. Regarding the first point let us refer to Dr. Bradford's "Law of Scattering." Wood says that it "implies that only a third, approximately, of the articles relevant to a given subject field are published in journals relating specifically to that field."[8]

A great deal has been done just within the last few years to decrease

---

[7] Stanley D. Truelson, "What the *Index Medicus* Indexes and Why." *Medical Library Association Bulletin*, LIV (October, 1966), p. 330.

[8] N. W. Wood, "Abstracts and Their Indexes—Style, Presentation and Uses," *Aslib Proceedings*, XVIII (June, 1966), p. 166.

the time lag between submission, publication and abstracting. For example in the APA study referred to by Hathaway and Pike, it was stated that as of December, 1964, the average interval between submission and publication was about nine months.[9] Now, as of January, 1966, *Psychological Abstracts* has computerized its operations, and reduced the time lag to three or four months. This same pattern can be cited in several other information services, notably *Index Medicus*, in which several years ago 80 percent of its items were six months old. And as of the most recent study in December, 1965, only 20 percent of its items were six months old.[10] Even this much represents a challenge to be corrected, though, and one could almost say that speed of delivery is the most important single element in producing abstracting journals. It also means, unfortunately, that for the time being quality must simply be subordinated to high-speed dissemination. Researchers and librarians will be alerted of a great wealth of material, but no machine can alert them of the best to be had— not yet, at least.

Considering all that has been discussed here, poor Pike's proposal seems somehow way out in left field. That he has zest for his work is laudable, but that he should want to compete against ERIC and *Education Index* is almost laughable. Let him get on the bandwagon like all the rest, and forever leave his mark on Abbotsford State University by helping to strengthen national, rather local information services in education. Waiting for the computer to be commonplace in libraries, as Hathaway suggests, is not as far-fetched as it may seem. But first, computerized information storage and retrieval will have to be perfected by larger, and mostly national systems.

Bibliography

Astin, Alexander W. and Panos, Robert J. "A Data Bank for Research on Higher Education," *The Educational Record*, XLVII (Winter, 1966), 5-17.

Bry, Ilse and Afferbach, Lois. "Bibliographical Challenges in the Age of the Computer," *Library Journal*, XC (February 15, 1965), 813-818.

Burchinal, Lee G. "ERIC, and the Need to Know," *NEA Journal*, LVI (February, 1967), 65-72.

---

[9] Garvey and Griffith, p. 1656.

[10] Mary F. Jackson, "The *Index Medicus:* Why It Works and When It Doesn't," Medical Library Association Bulletin, LIV (October, 1966), p. 326.

Dolby, J. L. "University Libraries and the Information Needs of the Researcher: A Consumer's View," *Aslib Proceedings,* XVIII (July, 1966), 185-190.

Foskett, D. J. *Classification and Indexing in the Social Sciences.* London: Butterworth & Co., Ltd., 1963.

Garvey, William D. and Griffith, Belver C. "Scientific Information Exchange in Psychology," *Science,* CXLVI (December 25, 1964), 1655-59.

"Indexers to be Recruited by ERIC," *Wilson Library Bulletin,* XLI (September, 1966), 19.

Jackson, Mary F. "The *Index Medicus:* Why It Works and When It Doesn't," *Medical Library Association Bulletin,* LIV (October, 1966), 325-328.

Kister, Kenneth. "The Literature of the Social and Behavioral Sciences," *Choice,* III (April, 1966), 99-102.

Line, M. B. "University Libraries and the Information Needs of the Researcher: A Provider's View," *Aslib Proceedings,* XVIII (July, 1966), 178-784.

Shaw, Ralph. "Integrated Bibliography," *Library Journal,* XC (February 15, 1965), 819-822.

Truelson, Stanley D. "What the *Index Medicus* Indexes and Why," *Medical Library Association Bulletin,* LIV (October, 1966), 329-336.

Uytterschaut, L. "Literature Searching Methods in Social Science Research: A Pilot Inquiry," *The American Behavioral Scientist,* IX (May, 1966), 14.

Wasserman, Paul. *The Librarian and the Machine.* Detroit: Gale Research Co., 1965.

White, Carl H. *Sources of Information in the Social Sciences.* Totowa, New Jersey: Bedminster Press, 1964.

Wood, N. W. "Abstracts and Their Indexes—Style, Presentation and Uses, *Aslib Proceedings,* XVIII (June, 1966), 160-166.

SAMPLE ANALYSIS / II
By Virginia R. Clark

The question raised by Mr. Pike's proposal to establish a modest abstracting service for the users of his library in the Education field have been investigated with ambiguous results. How do scholars and scientists satisfy their information needs? Mr. Voigt, in his study of scientists' approaches to information[1] defined three types of needs. Some of the confusions arising in the discussion between Mr. Pike and Mr. Hathaway are due to failure to distinguish these types. Voigt found that scientists need to keep abreast of the literature in the field, a need he called *current*; they need immediate information, an *everyday* need; and on rare occasions they need to search the entire literature on a subject, a need he labelled *exhaustive*. His and other similar surveys show that Mr. Hathaway is right in saying that the primary method for keeping up with the literature and satisfying everyday needs is through informal conversation, exchange at meetings, and perusing the literature as it comes out; he is equally right in thinking that graduate students about to embark on thesis work need an exhaustive survey of the literature, but he is on very shaky ground when he asserts that abstracts, especially of the modest sort Mr. Pike is proposing, would not be used.

A use survey of the bibliographic needs of social and behavioral scientists demonstrates the great variety among the scholars of different disciplines in their use of abstracts: psychologists use *Psychological Abstracts* 100 percent; anthropologists use *Sociological Abstracts* about 50 percent and among economists, most use *Journal of Economics Abstracts* 90 percent) and less frequently *Economic Abstracts* (35 percent).[2] The death rate of abstracting services in education, the most recent victim being *Education Abstracts* (UNESCO) in 1965, suggests that education scholars may fail to use abstracts. However, before basing a decision on this, one should consider the difference between a large general abstract covering a wide and complex field and probably many months behind in its coverage and a small selective abstracting service covering material

---

[1] Voigt, Melvin J. *Scientists' Approaches to Information.* Chicago: American Library Association, 1961.

[2] Appel, John S. and T. Gurr. "Bibliographic Needs of Social and Behavioral Scientists: Report of a Pilot Survey," *American Behavioral Scientist* (June, 1964), 51-54.

received in the scholar's own library and as up-to-date as a new book list.

There are some further questions that require investigation. Does the advisability of Mr. Pike's proposed abstracting service depend upon the adequacy of the present indexing, abstracting and reviewing services in the education field? Does *Education Index* merit Mr. Pike's criticism? Will ERIC (Educational Research Information Center) materials actually perform the services expected? Are forthcoming books being adequately reviewed in the journals? Is this material easily accessible to Mr. Pike's readers?

Since 1961, *Education Index* has no longer provided an author index nor included books and pamphlets; it is now a subject index only. It does include government publications of selected agencies, but does not index foreign publications. There is very little time-lag, usually about two months, between publication date of the article and receipt of the index by the reader.

Books are reviewed in several journals, but these are actually a small fraction of "books received." In the quarterly *Harvard Educational Review*, there are long, discursive, critical, scholarly reviews; other journals such as *Teachers College Record* do the long comparative review, while others such as the *Journal of Higher Education* offer the more conventional short review. Recent research is well covered in the *Journal of Educational Research* and the *Review of Educational Research*, although the latter, by treating each of ten or so topics thoroughly in cycles, may exhibit a three-year gap between earlier and later treatments.

ERIC has provided an extensive listing of 1,740 documents relating to the educational problems of the disadvantaged. Each of ten categories such as dropouts, talent loss, remedial reading, etc, is introduced by a 500-word summary usually by a newspaper reporter of a representative program, followed by a list of document numbers of related programs. The documents corresponding to these numbers are then abstracted in a reduced format of very fine print. There is also a name index, a documents-number index, and a subject index of key words. The latter enables the investigator to search and group documents in accordance with his interests. Documents are available at a price in both microfiche and "hardcover" form.[3]

---

[3] U. S. Dept. of Health, Education, and Welfare. ERIC, Educational Research Information Center. *Catalog of Selected Documents on the Disadvantaged*. Washington, D. C., 1966.

All educators should be acquainted with programs in all ten categories. For these, ERIC performs an important and indispensable function and no effort has been spared to render the documents accessible from every research point of view.

The presence of all of these quite excellent tools still begs our original question: does their existence obviate the need for Mr. Pike's proposed abstracting service? Do they not imply a still further process of selection and of actually obtaining the material and placing it in the hands of the scholar?

Indeed, Mr. Pike's modest proposal merely extends the normal function of the librarian: to select materials of interest to the reader, to inform him of their existence, and to make provision for his receipt of them—tasks which every reference librarian must accomplish in practically every reference encounter. By formalizing these tasks in print, including descriptions of new reference and indexing tools, their potentialities, and how they work; by including the call number of books just cataloged and the references to vital journal articles, especially in the foreign journals, Mr. Pike is actually proposing to short cut the effort of both reader and librarian. The few hours spent in producing this bulletin which is actually an expanded version of a new books list and a modest journal indexing service, will be saved for Mr. Pike and his readers by permitting the latter to by-pass card catalog searching, the scanning of journals for articles of interest, and personal instruction in the use of ERIC and other new research tools, and to go directly to the materials of interest to them.

The advantages of Mr. Pike's personal contact with the faculty are important. Mr. Pike has already been doing some selective dissemination of information to professors and he is merely proposing to systematize and formalize what he is already doing.

Mr. Hathaway has not taken into consideration the fact that the use potential of such a personalized service in the field of the social sciences, and particularly education, is not known. Much work has been done regarding its value in the area of science and technology, especially in engineering and industrial libraries where it is termed "dissemination services."[4] S. Herner, for example, discusses the preparation of a selected reading list for an Applied Physics Laboratory which "cites under proper subject headings all articles in the 200 journals taken that have a bearing

---

[4] Schutze, Gertrude. *Documentation Source Book.* New York: Scarecrow Press, 1965.

upon the activities of the Laboratory and its staff." He estimates that it should not take up more than ten hours of the librarian's time and seven of the typist's.[5] While this does not involve abstracts, most articles are preceded by abstracts and the writing of short indicative abstracts, which seem to me the most valuable in this context, takes very little time for an intelligent subject specialist. And while the need for rapid dissemination of published material is not pressing in the education field, the service relieves the reader of many hours' work, of great importance in this era of work-time pressures. It also would relieve Mr. Pike of certain repetitive reference chores.

This type of abstract bulletin was quite popular in the 1940's and 1950's, before the advent of computers on a large scale. Since the appearance of computerized indexes, it has been assumed that there is no longer a function for this personal service except in documents libraries. However, Verner W. Clapp has suggested that the new methods of "information retrieval" are adding to the libraries' burden "by increasing the quantities of material for which they must take responsibility. . . . The computers are facilitating the production of index-type books and periodicals which libraries must possess in order to give good service."[6] Obviously, informing the staff of these tools and instructing them in their use consumes the reference librarian's time unless he can distribute printed informational material.

Recently, Menzel[7] has found a tendency to revert to the abstract, with a strong emphasis on personal communication, suggesting that a selective abstracting service in newsletter format including inside information usually disseminated among a select few, notes of meetings, etc., might be welcomed. Bergen[8] in discussing the possible disrupting effect of trying to "formalize the informal and informalize the formal" methods of communication, seems to be suggesting that if carefully done, it would represent a real contribution. Mr. Pike's proposal, adapted to both these goals and kept within the limited radius of his own and closely related university departments, might serve a useful function.

---

[5] Herner, S. "The Selected Reading List: A Means of Improving the Use of Periodical Literature," *Special Libraries*, XLI (1950), 324-326; 335-336.

[6] Clapp, Verner W. " 'Information Storage and Retrieval' and the Problems of Libraries," *American Documentation*, XII (July, 1961), 224-226.

[7] Menzel, Herbert. "The Information Needs of Current Scientific Research," *Library Quarterly*, XXXIV (January, 1964), 4-9.

[8] Bergen, Daniel. "Bibliographic Organization in the Social Sciences," *Wilson Library Bulletin*, XL (April, 1966), 751-58.

Regarding Mr. Hathaway's wish to wait for the computer, at least in terms of special dissemination services within the university, Wasserman[9] suggests that computerized bibliographic control is much further in the future than most librarians realize. Most computerized Selective Dissemination of Information (SDI) systems within institutions function most efficiently in situations involving a large number of report documents and many research personnel in a rapidly developing research and development situation.[10] In education, on the other hand, it would seem more important to keep abreast of the main aspects of the field in a more modest and selective way. But even if Mr. Pike's experiment should prove a failure, it will yield valuable information on this whole unexplored area of user studies.[11]

John Markus[12] brings those dreaming of the new computer index utopia down to earth with a realistic appraisal of the economics of computerized indexes. Because of their high cost, individuals cannot purchase them but must use them in libraries. The library market is relatively small. Mr. Markus points out that *Engineering Index* has a press run of only about 1,500 copies for its annual volume which sells for $75. Permuted-title indexes are often able to cover costs, but in general Mr. Markus suggests that the government may have to enter this field in order to prevent the price from becoming prohibitive. The higher the price of the index the fewer the purchasers, since smaller libraries must go without. Probably the most successful of all computerized indexes is the government-published *Index Medicus* with its attendant selective computerized bibliography service, MEDLARS. It is noteworthy that the new computerized index issued by ERIC is a government publication. The success of privately published indexes involves consideration of economics and need. A field like education may as yet be unable to support a really comprehensive computerized index. Hence, Mr. Hathaway's suggestion to "wait for the computer" in this field may be a rash and careless one.

A distinct aspect of interest in this case is the interplay of the person-

---

[9] Wasserman, Paul. *The Librarian and the Machine*. Detroit, Michigan: Gale, 1963.
[10] Special Libraries Association Meeting with Simmons College Students. Visit to Sylvania, Waltham, Mass. Lecture and demonstration of SDI, February 18, 1967.
[11] Davis, Richard A. *Bibliography of Use Studies*. Drexel Institute of Technology, Graduate School of Library Science, Philadelphia, May, 1964. Since this is annotated, it provides a good idea of some of the results of use studies among social scientists.
[12] Markus, John. "State of the Art of Published Indexes," *American Documentation*, XIII (January, 1962), 15-23; 23-30.

alities involved and questions of administration and personnel management. If we are to believe in the significance of the "cigarette ploys" in
the early action of this case, Mr. Pike's personality is revealed as pas-
sive, dependent, and immature, lacking in self-confidence and self-as-
sertiveness. In presenting himself for Mr. Hathaway's encouragement, he
has taken a step forward toward developing independence and initiative by offering to undertake what, at the very least, cannot fail to be an
interesting use study and which should not cost much in either time,
personnel or materials.

What obligation does a supervisor have to "develop" a bright subordinate whose development may be dependent upon his encouragement?
We suspect that undertaking his abstracting project may open the way
for Mr. Pike to begin his long-delayed Ph. D. work, since it may unblock
an inhibition against independent work and enable him to begin to translate his dream into a reality. What benefit will Mr. Hathaway and the
university derive from this if Mr. Pike moves up and transfers to a higher
position elsewhere? Does a senior librarian have obligations to the
standards of librarianship as a profession, even though his efforts in encouraging and training a subordinate may result in his protégé outstripping his mentor and ultimately leaving the library perhaps poorer in
terms of personnel by his departure?

Does Mr. Hathaway's negative response to Mr. Pike's proposal arise
from reasoned judgment or is it a direct consequence of passivity and
timidity engendered by the recent unfortunate episode in the university?
How can Mr. Hathaway be sure his judgment is not clouded by envy of
the vitality and youthful enthusiasm of Mr. Pike? Has Mr. Hathaway given
consideration to the effect of his discouraging attitude on this young
man's subsequent development and career? Perhaps the encouragement
and development of Mr. Pike's initiative is more important than the
modest cost of this abstracting service, even if it should be a total failure.
Is Mr. Hathaway himself mature enough to realize that every investiga-
ive effort in an unknown area, whether a success or failure, yields new
knowledge? Can he communicate this to Mr. Pike, if Mr. Pike carries out
his idea and faces failure? Is he generous enough to encourage Mr. Pike
to continue his doctoral studies even though this means that academically
Mr. Pike will "go above" him?

If he is able to be so generous, perhaps he will be rewarded by
catching something of the enthusiasm and "openness" of Mr. Pike's at-

titude; perhaps it will cure the tinge of disillusionment, defeatism and withdrawal that has resulted from the university scandal. These peripheral considerations are not by any means least important and librarians must take them into account in every decision involving the initiative of subordinate personnel.

SAMPLE ANALYSIS / III
By C. M. Keen Jr.

The basic problem posed in this case is that of the best tool-in-trade for a divisional faculty, the School of Education, of a large state university. The graduate school of education has about 270 students working for some higher degree. Presumably they do research. Original? To be called *Waiting for the Computer: or Pike's Peak Proposal Busted.*

CHAPTER I

In Which Morgan Pike Proposes a New Processing Tool

As a subject specialist with a library degree Morgan Pike is made aware of a bibliographical deficiency. His brief experience at Abbotsford University causes him to believe that there is room for some creative library activity in the field of education. Therefore, he proposes to write and/or edit a monthly abstract of Abbotsford's education acquisitions. His analysis of the lack of such a good tool seems to be well founded.[1] A question might be asked, however, about the implied value for Abbotsford University of abstracting *foreign* literature. Could it not be that these graduate students can make good academic progress by depending solely upon English language, if not only U.S., publications? This because of the very nature of American methods and standards in education training.

Morgan's reasons for his proposal were commendable. The project "planned" was to be (1) a library service to his academic community (2) a library tool which other libraries might use (3) of public relations value to the university. This may not be 'corny' because such a venture if successful would prove to be a shot in the arm after adverse publicity on the issue of academic freedom. Moreover, such a project might improve the public image of the *state* institution in comparison to "better" private academic institutions.

---

[1] His general remarks about *Education Abstracts* and *Education Index* are borne out by an examination of these. See also the notations in Winchell and Carl White (*Sources of Information in the Social Sciences*).

Pike's job demands that he *know* the literature in his field and he must have certain time free for reading and browsing. His technique of notifying instructors of items of interest is commendable. Initiative is shown. He evidently knows his faculty. He isn't sitting waiting for his customers to approach! Pike's proposal is poorly planned because he doesn't utilize the available documentation in his discussion with his boss. More of this later. But Pike does have a clear picture of what he wants to do. Unlike Hathaway he defines "abstract " as a "summary," meaning not only bibliographic entry and index, but more precisely as a synopsis or brief precis of the item.[2] Moreover, he has tested his idea on one teacher with a favorable response. It would be important to know what others thought. Here he is vulnerable. Why not quiz the other teachers? Hathaway evidently doesn't place much faith in Morgan Pike's education degree—perhaps with some justification. Many a "master of education" has received a degree without grappling with the broad field of education literature. Perhaps Pike's interest has focused on such subjects as "An Analysis of Reading Habits of Fifth Graders in Stoneham, Massachusetts" or an "An Examination of the Reliability of Grading Scales used in Amarillo, Texas." The library degree is a better indicator of familiarization with the literature in the field than the education degree.

On the subject of *selectivity* Pike seems to have the better argument. ERIC collects selectivity. Information retrieval via computer services has to be this way. The key is in the "descriptors" or machine readable subject headings which are used.[3] These need to be both sufficiently precise so as to exclude non-relevant materials and yet sufficiently inclusive so as to make coverage complete. It is precisely here that the need for more Pikes is apparent. ERIC frankly depends on the subject specialist by

---

[2] See A. Resnick, "Relative Effectiveness of Document Titles and Abstracts for Determining Relevance of Documents", *Science*, Vol. 134, (Oct. 6, 1961) pp. 1004-1005. The author examined the field of physics and found "no significant difference between titles and abstracts." Another conclusion may be important: on specific questions abstracts were found to be significantly better especially when the purpose is "to notify research workers of availability of documents which might be relevant to their work interests . . ."

[3] *Research in Education*, December, 1966. The same problem is illustrated in Universal Reference System's volumes on *Political Science*. Harold Borko says, "The detailed tasks of document analysis are indexing, classification, abstracting, and foreign-language translation." Harold Borko, "The Storage and Retrieval of Educational Information," *The Journal of Teacher Education* Vol. XV, Number 4, December, 1964, p. 451.

appealing for the same to "feed information" to its new Clearinghouse Centers.[4] Without such the input to the machine will be faulty. Pike ought to look for a job with ERIC!

CHAPTER II

In Which Charles Hathaway Disposed of the Disquisition

The Coordinator of Reference and Research Services must be of old Yankee stock if not a personal emigrant to the southwest. Good old (?) careful, cautious, conservative Charlie! His attitude of "wait and see" for tomorrow and tomorrow and tomorrow creeps on this petty pace . . . is all too often typical of the Yankee, if not old librarians. Hathaway probably never had an original idea. The world of Morgans will soon pass him by. Cautious Charlie is afraid of experimentation in his library and uses what knowledge he possesses to stifle staff initiative. Just what is he coordinating anyway? Can he veto the Pike proposal? Is there a Reference Librarian to whom Pike can appeal?

Hathaway is generally correct on professional techniques they "talk" through "informal channels" for getting the word around on printed literature.[5] The big question is, though: Is this the best and most effective method for research *scholars?* The answer? No. There is no longer any reason or virtue in spending time to walk over ground already covered. In fact, it has been established that "it is far more expensive to repeat research than to search . . . by computers."[6] We should be skeptical of the assertion that these same scholars do not *like* bibliographic tools. This may be an impression of Charlie's not grounded in fact. However,

---

[4] *Research in Education,* December, 1966, inside rear page. See also Borko's "Analysis of the Problem" in the article cited above (p. 451).

[5] Personal observation after sixteen years of college teaching and participation in professional conferences. A personal check of various theses references for such bibliographical aids proved 100 percent fruitless. The American Psychological Association research is discussed and reported by William D. Garvey and Belver C. Griffith in two articles:

"Research Frontier: The APA Projection Scientific Information Exchange in Psychology", *Journal of Consulting Psychology,* Vol. 10, 1963, pp. 297-302 and in "Scientific Information Exchange in Psychology", *Science,* Vol. 146, (Dec. 25, 1964) pp. 1655-59. Whether or not the principles mentioned here would apply to education is a moot question.

[6] B. L. Hazeltine, "Information Explosion", *Science Teacher,* February, 1965, p. 27.

the attitude is unimportant. I may not *like* airplanes or elevators but I still travel cross-continent via air and take the elevator ten floors up! Both sure beat walking! Ergo: don't research scholars, even the absent minded, use *some* tools? The assertion that scholars don't use such tools may mean that scholars he knows don't use those tools in the reference room of his library. They may go elsewhere or have research grants which provide personal copies.

We might well question Hathaway's use of his experience with teachers who did not use either *Historical Abstracts* or *Economic Abstracts*. These had been started only a decade ago, *Historical Abstracts* in 1954 and *Economic Abstracts* in 1953, and might have been so new to Hathaway's friends that their usefulness was unproven. Or could Hathaway have forgotten that he talked to his teacher-friends *before* these journals were born? Was Hathaway aware that these aids might not have met the specific needs of his scholarly friends? The historians may have been interested in local history or narrow specialists within the United States' field. The economists might have felt that the scope of *Economic Abstracts* published by New York University was too limited and that the same title published in the Hague was weak in American entries and contained poorly chosen subject headings.

Hathaway's heady recommendation of *Index Medicus* is fine—under certain conditions. The basic requirements for such a service are: (1) A single large center with almost unlimited (complete) acquisitions in the subject field. (2) A large and *pressing* demand for *immediate* access to the latest research, (including foreign data). In medicine this demand may be a case of life or death for medical patrons. (3) A requirement to have access to *all* that leaders in the field are writing. (4) An acceptable list of subject headings. (5) Finances to operate the high speed digital computers and to print a large number of the 'catalogs' produced.

Without such requirements being present in the field of education it is doubtful if the computer will find a maximal role in bibliographic control of educational materials. Certainly it will not be "commonplace" in libraries. *Index Medicus* is not.

Both Pike and Hathaway missed several points in the APA study. The first is that researchers *do* use the tools at their disposal. Secondly, the study may not have too much validity for an academic community because it was done with APA members, not all of whom were in education or research. Third, the study revealed that only 1 percent of psychologists read 50 percent of the articles in the "core" journals, not that these men lacked time to read.[7] A study is needed before we can assume educational researchers are the same as or different from psychologists.[8]

CHAPTER III

In Which We Counsel the Chief Librarian of Abbotsford University

CONFIDENTIAL MEMO: TO: Chief Librarian

SUBJECT: Pike's Proposal to Abstract Education Materials

A. Encourage Mr. Pike

(1) Have him query, on an informal basis, other School of Education professors. After this is done get a written response to a formalized questionnaire.

(2) Permit Pike to begin his task on a limited basis. Great oaks from little acorns—yes, even DDC began this way! He will discover that 15 hours per week may be insufficient time to do a serviceable job. If success comes prepare to expand.

(3) Give Pike the use of a secretary to transcribe and distribute the summary-abstract to faculty. Have "ditto" copies available in conspicuous places for the graduate students. Tabulate responses. Actual use of the same will quickly establish whether or not faculty and students will use the new tool!

(4) The principle of selectivity has favorable and weak points. Discuss these with both Pike and Hathaway. Selectivity is good if based on the needs and demands of the Abbotsford community. No one service can be definitive and to make it too comprehensive will at first defeat its purpose. Selectivity will also assist the avoidance of duplication of other's works. However, the narrower the scope of selection, say 40 journals, the less value it has in the long run for the people using the serv-

---

[7] *Science,* Vol. 146, p. 1658.

[8] The same is true for principles developed in scientific analysis of which a great deal of computer work is being done. To date little or no indication is available as to the results of a National Science Foundation research grant to the Air Force "concerned with the application of mathematics and computer-age technology in storing and using information." *Wilson Library Bulletin,* January, 1966, p. 407.

ice. Scholars and librarians may prefer complete subject coverage. The selectivity factor will become increasingly important if the tool grows and is used in other schools or public libraries. (If it looks successful contact Gale Research in Detroit. Wouldn't *Pike's Abbotsford University Abstracts* look good?)

B. Observe Mr. Hathaway

(1) What are his attitudes to library service?

(2) Is his reading current as part of his own job function? Does he read at all? When Hathaway spoke about "information retrieval" he was evidently unaware that the U. S. Office of Education project begun in November, 1966 utilizes the computer. The Office's Bureau of Research created thirteen Educational Research Information Centers (ERIC)[9] to supply monthly research findings for its *Research in Education* journal. The journal carries two main types of data, reports and projects, which are subdivided into "Resumes" (abstracts) and "Indexes". Interested parties can purchase the "Reports" from ERIC Document Reproduction Service at Bell & Howell in Cleveland whereas "Projects" documents are not available. A comparison of the sample "print out" facing page one of the Report Resumes bears a striking resemblance to the "print out" in *Wilson Library Bulletin*,[10] mentioned in connection with science computer operations. Evidently education learned from science.

(3) Sound him out in staff meetings on personnel relations. Suggest that he ask Pike to produce some sample abstracts and to investigate further, including in such investigation work on computers.[11] Pike should note the time involved in writing and editing the abstracts.

---

[9] *Research in Education*, December, 1966, inside front and rear pages. The Centers are in California, New Mexico, Oregon, Ohio, Indiana, Michigan and New York. Each collects data relating to a special phase of education. For example, the clearinghouse in New Mexico carries the reports on "Small Schools and Rural Compensatory Education."

[10] *Research in Education*, December, 1966, unnumbered page and also *Wilson Library Bulletin,* December, 1966. p. 398.

[11] Was he aware of F. B. Baker's "Use of Computers in Educational Research," *Review of Educational Research*, December, 1963, pp. 572-573, or M. F. Tauber's "Documentation Activities of Associations," *Wilson Library Bulletin*, May, 1964, pp. 768-772? Some work is being done on information retrieval in adult education as well as at the high school level. See R. DeCrow "Library of Continuing Educa-

(4) Ask Hathaway to study the problem of education abstracting and present his conclusions to you.[12] WE WANT ACTION!

C. Conclusion

The literature on documentation and information retrieval, as well as the practical everyday use of computers, as observed recently by Simmons Library School guests of the Boston branch of Special Libraries Association at Sylvania Electronics plant, suggests they are optimally used in the natural sciences where industrial and educational activity is connected. Population centers, like the Atlantic coast megalopolis, induce a wide *demand* for information control centers by multiple academic and/or commercial institutions. In this connection, the location of ERIC Centers is significant. All are in large urban areas. Computer application to the social sciences, like education, needs both further experimentation and study.

The following titles channeled my thinking:

Foskett, D.J. *Information Service in Libraries,* Philosophical Library, Inc., New York, c. 1961. Stress on role of natural sciences.

Harvey, Joan M. ed. *Information Methods of Research Workers in the Social Sciences,* Library Association, London, 1961. Chapters I and II on the "Advanced Research Worker" and "Research Student."

---

tion," *Adult Leadership,* December, 1964, p. 180 and L. H. Freiser "Toronto's Answer to Automated Information," *Phi Delta Kappan,* June, 1963, p. 444. A single issue of the *Wilson Library Bulletin* (May, 1964) concentrates on this problem. He might find some help in "APA Instructions for the Preparation of Abstracts" *American Psychologist,* Vol. 16 (1961) p. 833. D. J. Foskett, "Information Problems in the Social Sciences with Special Reference to Mechanization" *ASLIB Proceedings,* 17:328 (December, 1965).

[12] Any number of articles are helpful here. These bear directly:

a) "Cooperative Educational Abstracting Service Planned," *UNESCO Bulletin for Libraries,* 20:44 (January, 1966).

b) "Push Button Bibliography Today and Tomorrow" by K. R. Shaffer, *Bulletin of Bibliography,* 24:73-8 (May, 1964).

c) "Abstracts and Their Indexes" by N. W. Wood *ASLIB Proceedings,* 18:160-166 (June, 1966).

d) John S. Andrews, "10 years of Indexing: the British Education Index (1954-1963), *Library Association Record,* May, 1964, pp. 203-206. Compares theirs to *Education Index;* used same subject headings.

e) William H. Huff, "Indexing, Abstracting, and Translation Services," *Library Trends,* Vol. 10, p. 427 (January, 1962). This whole issue is devoted to "Current Trends in U. S. Periodical Publishing."

f) Arthur M. Bodin, "A Proposal for New Bibliographic Tools . . .," *Journal of Counseling Psychology,* 1963, Vol. 10, pp. 193-197.

Huff suggests that ". . . the greater reliance of fields (such as social sciences) upon materials other than serials seems to point up an inadequacy in indexing-abstracting services," *"Ibid.,* p. 429.

Kent, Allen. *Textbook on Mechanized Information Retrieval*, 2nd ed., New York, Interscience Publishers, 1966.

Meadow, Charles T. *The Analysis of Information Systems*, New York, John Wiley & Sons, Inc., 1967.

Sharp, Harold S. ed., *Readings in Information Retrieval*, New York, Scarecrow Press, Inc., 1964. Section VII on abstracting.

Shera, Jesse H. *Library Science and Documentation*, New York, Interscience Publishers, 1967.

Taube, Mortimer. *Computers and Common Sense*, New York, Columbia University Press, 1961. Subtitled "The Myth of the Thinking Machine". Stresses human roles.

Wasserman, Paul. *The Librarian and the Machine*, Detroit, Gale Research Co., c. 1965. Chapter IX on "Attitudes", Chapter X on "Key Issues." Discusses KWIC, SDI, etc.

SAMPLE ANALYSIS / IV

By Paul L. Brawley

Pike's Position

Mr. Pike, a young man who does not seem to have much "cool," thinks "it would be a good idea to try getting out some kind of abstract of the educational literature" received in his library. There is a need for a good publication of this kind—not the one which he proposes however. His remarks about *Education Index* can be accepted but not in the light that they do any discredit to the index. Pike ignores Enoch Pratt Library's *Educational books of (the year)* which is "a thorough listing of books, pamphlets, monographs, yearbooks and issues of magazines which appeared the previous year and are devoted to a single topic in education."[1] His comment that students in education "could make use of" an education abstract is acceptable. He does correctly state one of the conclusions of the American Psychological Association's study of information exchange. It is also true that UNESCO's *Education Abstracts*, which devotes each issue to articles on a specific subject in various countries, has not been as successful or as useful as UNESCO's bibliographies in the social sciences. However, beyond these few points of relative agreement, I find little else with which I do not take issue.

The Educational Research Information Center (ERIC) limits itself to current research in education and particularly educational information about the disadvantaged. Out of every five documents, considered for inclusion, only two are eventually selected.[2] This is an extremely selective process. However, as it doesn't cover the same material that Pike has in mind, he generalizes that "it's not selective enough." And "our people" at Abbotsford had better get used to microfiche P.D.Q.

Pike obviously has no idea how much larger this abstracting job is than he suggests. For example, the *International Economics Selections Bibliography*, which is published quarterly by the Department of Economics at the University of Pittsburgh, *annotates* new English language books in

---

[1] Carl M. White, *Sources of Information in the Social Sciences* (Totowa, New Jersey: The Bedminster Press Inc., 1964), p. 339.

[2] Lee G. Burchinal and Harold A. Haswell, "How to Put Two and a Half Tons of Research Into One Handy Little Box," *American Education* (February, 1966), pp. 23-25.

economics as well as selected titles in French, German, Spanish, Italian, and Polish. *IESB* also publishes a supplement, *IESB Series 2*, which appears once a year and contains annotations of books in a special field or subdiscipline of economics. At present *IESB* annotates between 260 and 290 books every quarter. The annotations are provided by an Economics Department of 27 professors, associate professors and assistant professors and published by an editorial staff of three. Pike is suggesting that he alone "concisely abstract"—not merely annotate—selected, not simply books but, "articles, books, government publications, yearbooks, and so on." He plans first to mimeograph it *once a month* and then perhaps prepare it for publication by the university press. This could easily become a full time job; to simply read all the material he is hoping to abstract could take most of his working time; if he plans to merely scan the material he will not be able to "concisely abstract" it. Ten to fifteen hours a week might be a reasonable figure if he were merely editing such a publication. Also he would definitely need a staff with more than ten hours a week to carry out the mechanics of publication. He has also forgotten that he will have to provide a subject index to this proposed publication, if he expects it to be useful; and in all probability he will have to devise a classified arrangement of some sort.

What Pike fails to realize is that he is not qualified for such an undertaking. As far as the scholar or professor in education is concerned his "master's in ed" is nothing more than a drop in the bucket. He may "keep up" with what is happening in the field, but he is not actively involved in the field; and therefore he is not aware of what is going on before he reads it in the journals. On the other hand scholars and teachers are creating the articles in the journals and are often aware of information contained in such articles months before the articles appear.[3] Pike may be aware of the most important names, but isn't this boast really small potatoes? And is Pike qualified to abstract journals and books in all of the major foreign languages? No, there's nothing for it: Pike is not the man for the job! Hathaway hits the nail on the head when he remarks that scholars and professors wouldn't give a damn about Pike's abstracts—partially because he is *merely* a librarian, but mainly because he is unqualified.

Pike implies that bibliographic control is not too *hot* in education or

[3] William D. Garvey and Belver C. Griffith, "Scientific Information Exchange in

Psychology," *Science* (December 25, 1964), p. 1655.

in any of the social sciences. Certainly no one will argue that point! Librarians and researchers are experiencing mounting frustration with the tidal wave of publications and trying to cope with it with inadequate bibliographic tools.[4] Education particularly seems to be lacking a publication on the level of *Psychological Abstracts* or *Historical Abstracts*. To reiterate: there is a need for a *good* abstracting journal, but what Pike is proposing—a local, shoddy, mimeographed affair—would not only go unused, but would be a bibliographic disgrace—a waste of his and the library's time. Bibliographic control in the social sciences is bad, yes, but a philosophy that "something is better than nothing" can only lead to bibliographic disaster.

What Pike might consider important and include in his *selective* tool might not be at all what a number of instructors or scholars might put into such a publication. Pike queries, "Until computers *become* commonplace, isn't some sort of *selective* control necessary? Doesn't the great increase of publication—in all fields and subfields—require selectivity?"

"Yes, Mr. Pike, yes!! But in all the fields and subfields of education, in all the various languages—with all the various degrees of emphasis, interpretation and controversy—are *you* expecting *us* to choose *you* to do our selecting for us?"

"My primary interest, Mr. Pike, is education of mentally retarded children; my esteemed colleague with the mauve polkadot bow tie is concerned with experiments in computer tutoring; and my charming colleague in the chartreuse mini-skirt and bright yellow slingbacks, who is deliciously sucking on her lower lip, is only interested in electric shock as an inducement to learning. Can your selective abstracts of fifty or sixty journals do anything for us all? Don't bother to answer!"

Pike has not given this whole project more than an elementary "thinking-through." It's no wonder the director turned him down cold.

Hathaway's Position

This man is obviously the 007 of the case—not only does he have cigarettes, but he is able to produce a smart lighter *prestissimo*. As Pike explained his abstract Hathaway listened very patiently; his questions

---

[4] Lewis C. Branscomb, "Libraries in Larger Institutions of Higher Education," *The Future of Library Service: Demographic Aspects and Implications*, ed. Frank L. Schick (Urbana, Illinois: University of Illinois Graduate School of Library Science, 1962), p. 183.

were short and to the point. Then seeing the absurdity of Pike's particular plan he very calmly and deliberately dropped his axe. It was a delightful administrative coup; his timing was flawless and designed to completely deflate our man Pike. Some may criticize Hathaway for being so blunt, but I rather think that sharp, incisive rap, that hammer-stroke blow, is part of being a competent administrator. If the man is bright, this quality can be most effective; if he is stupid, this can be disastrous.

Hathaway states, "Professors don't use abstracts and indexes—and all the other array of bibliographical utensils that have been developed. Most of their so-called "searching" is done . . . through informal channels—through a verbal exchange." Garvey and Griffith state that social scientists—teachers of social science included—with an emphasis on psychologists, do not depend even on journal articles, much less the later indexes and abstracts, for their informational needs. These "archival journals," bibliographies, indexes and abstracts are more for the student and the researcher.

The literature is only a portion of a system that encompasses many forms of information exchange; and without denying the great importance of archival journals it may be said that they have received a disproportionate share of the attentions being given to the mechanisms by which scientific information is disseminated.

In psychology at least, the exchanges of new scientific information between its principal producers and consumers does not wait upon journals. The active scientist, 40 percent of whom are employed in academic institutions, make use of a whole network of means of communication, many of them informal or of small range, and yet apparently highly efficient. Their efficiency lies not only in their expeditiousness but also in their selectivity, for the group that is actively interested in a particular set of findings is often quite small. Indeed, often the readership of a particular paper in a current journal may consist largely of people who already know its contents from earlier sources.[5]

Uytterschaut has found that scholars and even researchers are not very happy with existing bibliographic tools, dislike using them, and therefore do not depend on or use them to any great extent. "One may

---

[5] Garvey, p. 1655.

not conclude that the experienced research worker deliberately neglects the value of bibliographic tools. But as far as their practical use is concerned, he only consults them occasionally to fill in his knowledge of the documentation available in his nearest surroundings." Uytterschaut also pointed out that scholars and researchers do not really know how to go about investigating the literature of their fields; "one respondent actually mentioned that with any literature searching one has to pass through a period of 'trial and error.'" For many scholars it is a "hit or miss" affair.[6]

Paul Wasserman also notes that "there is the overpowering empirical evidence of generations of scholars and researchers, many of whom demonstrate their ineptness in the use of conventional library instruments."[7]

Uytterschaut also reveals the scholar's view of the reference librarian—or "documentalist" as he is called. In arriving at his conclusions Uytterschaut interviewed twenty scholars who had at one time or another engaged in social science research at the State University of Ghent. In addition to finding out how each scholar conducted his research, the interview dealt with the documentatlist's role in helping the scholar in his search.

Taking into consideration the dominant individual outlook of literature research, one may wonder whether the research worker thinks the searching can be taken to pieces and delegated in any part to a documentalist. Twelve of the respondents do think it is practicable and effective, whereas eight do not, except for the ancillary aspects of the searching or with the supposition that the documentalist can be considered a subject specialist. Even then, they felt it remains questionable. . . . The projected assistance does not cover very much. As a matter of fact, only seven percent would permit assistance in digging up literature sources and scanning classificatory headings. They think a documentalist can be charged to establish a reference list of documents suitable for investigating the given subject matter and summarize, not to abstract, the documents involved, but they deny unanimously that appropriate assistance could as a rule encompass marking relevant quotations, *abstracting* the material, or preparing a literature report.

---

[6] L. Uytterschaut, "Literature Searching Methods in Social Science Research: A Pilot Inquiry," *The American Behavioral Scientist* (May, 1966), p. 25.

[7] Paul Wasserman, *The Librarian and the Machine* (Detroit: Gale Research Co., 1965), p. 73.

The other 13 respondents normally would refuse to envisage that a documentalist would manage something useful independently, even upon a detailed instruction from the research worker.[8]

This bit of information would seem to point to the validity of Hathaway's statement that scholars would not trust "you—a librarian—to select the most important, the most significant material."

Now we come to "the real breakthrough"—the computer. Bergen states that "it is entirely possible that some time before the year 2,000 random access computer memories will be sizable enough to permit the storage of all the knowledge in the social sciences."[9] Branscomb notes that "automation comes slowly to libraries, but the librarian of the large research institution now admits that his outdated manual procedures are no longer appropriate to the tasks at hand."[10]

According to Wasserman most libraries are waiting to see how the experimental projects, which are working with computerized information retrieval, turn out before making any positive moves toward similar automation.[11] "The Western Reserve University Documentation and Communication Research Center is among other projects currently engaged in pioneering research and development of techniques and machines for storage and retrieval of educational research information."[12] Such committees as EDUCOM and COSTAL are presently engaged in planning for a national information network governed by a large computer center. At the Massachusetts Institute of Technology there are the computerized Information Transfer Experiments (INTREX), which have received international attention. Florida Atlantic University is also a pioneer in the large scale use of computers in a university library. And the list goes on and on and keeps growing each year. Even though a great number of libraries have automated as far as data processing goes, they are still wary of taking the step into information storage, transfer, and retrieval.

Hathaway's final comment, "Let's wait for the computer, what do you say?" is unfortunate. Somehow I think that this man who has displayed

---

[8] Uytterschaut, pp. 23-25.
[9] Dan Bergen, "Bibliographical Organization in the Social Sciences," *Wilson Library Bulletin* (April, 1966), p. 754.
[10] Branscomb, p. 183.
[11] Wasserman, pp. 125-126.
[12] Branscomb, p. 184.

such intelligence made a mistake by making this remark—whether he meant it or not. At best, Hathaway did not actually mean it—he intended it as a humorous gesture with which to end the interview. At worst he does not believe that bibliographic organization can be improved until the computer is commonplace in libraries. The truth is probably somewhere between the "best" and the "worst". At times Hathaway is quite erratic in his statements about information retrieval, abstracting and indexing, and the scholar's use of bibliographical tools. "It's my thought that information retrieval—locating relevant material on some subject—which is what we're talking about—is more a matter of verbal exchange than of abstracting and indexing." And yet he sees the computer, which demands *indepth* indexing, abstracting and cross references to a much greater degree than any existing bibliographical tools, as the panacea for our bibliographical problems. If scholars won't use present bibliographical tools what makes Hathaway think that they will embrace a tool compiled by a computer or be overjoyed at the prospect of learning how to conduct a meaningful dialog with a computer in order to gather bibliographical information? Does Hathaway expect the computer to stimulate an informal chat with a colleague? Certainly the computer can perform selective dissemination of information but this will be in the form of a printed list sent to each faculty member who has an "interest profile" stored in the computer. However, admitting that the computer will handle a great many operations, not even a sophisticated operation such as selective dissemination of information can provide a complete substitute "for the efficient librarian who can review the acquisition stream in a library and match this data with what he knows to be the exact and specific subject requirements of his clientele at exactly that moment in time."[13]

If the social sciences wish to take *Index Medicus* as its example, I should hope they would expand the scope somewhat to include more than journal articles. One must also take into consideration the fact that it is much easier to apply computer technology to the medical and physical sciences than to the less exact, more humanistic social and behavioral sciences.

The computer has already begun to completely revolutionize the important libraries in this country, and its effects will be felt even in the smallest libraries. Even though "a high degree of automation for every

---

[13] Wasserman, pp. 68-69.

academic library may never be financially justified, . . . state or regional centers will be established to serve as nerve centers from which information may be transmitted electronically to institutions within a particular area."[14] But as far as bibliographic control is concerned, an easy way out is "to wait for the computers;" however, there are those among us who think that something can be done for this generation of scholars and librarians—but it takes people who are willing to devote more than superficial attention to the matter.

A Possible Alternative

Although I believe Hathaway was correct to nip Pike's original proposal in the bud, he should have given some consideration to re-channelling Pike's enthusiasm and interest. Hathaway might suggest that Pike form the proverbial "committee" to investigate the possibilities or desirability of establishing a meaningful and useful abstracting journal of real excellence. This could be not Pike's baby but a publication and a product of the Department of Education and the University Library. Pike could be instrumental in getting such a publication going and possibly serve as its editor at first. In addition to the University of Pittsburgh many other universities sponsor publications of this sort. The faculty and perhaps some of the graduate students of the Department of Education could provide the abstracts or annotations, which would be submitted to an editor, who with a small staff could prepare it for press—perhaps on a quarterly basis. A really fine journal would be added prestige for the university and the Department of Education; in addition, relations could be greatly improved between the library and the faculty in the Department of Education.

---

[14] Branscomb, p. 184.

SAMPLE ANALYSIS / V
By Joan B. Shepardson

SCENE ONE

(Curtain rises on an unprepossessing living room in the home of Professor Montelle. There are a few stuffed chairs set carelessly about. A large brown painting broods over a fat sofa and the mood of the room seems to reflect the grey rainy day outside. There is a door to the kitchen at the rear; another at the side opens to admit a drenched Professor Montelle with young Mr. Morgan Pike in tow)

MONTELLE Whew! What a day! Martha? (*He throws his coat on a table*) Martha, you home? (*Silence*) Here, let me take your coat. Martha'll be here any minute. I called her before we left—she's probably gone out to get some nuts or something.

PIKE I do hope this isn't inconvenient for her—

MONTELLE Inconvenient?

PIKE Having me stop by for a drink like this.

MONTELLE Ha! Martha never considers a drink inconvenient!

PIKE Oh. (*He starts nervously looking in his pockets*)

MONTELLE Cigarette?

PIKE Thanks, I just don't seem to have mine with me.

(*The door swings open and Martha blows in clutching a large paper bag*)

MARTHA Sorry to be late boys. (*Sets down her bag with a clank*) We . . . ll, George, do introduce me to your luscious little friend.

MONTELLE (*Hastily*) Martha, this is Morgan Pike; he's in reference at the library.

PIKE How do you do, Mrs. Montelle. (*He extends a cautious hand*)

MARTHA I won't eat you, Morgy. I'm really quite harmless. (*She picks up George's coat*) Why don't you ever hang up your coat, you slob!

PIKE Perhaps I'd better run along, Professor Mon—

MONTELLE Sit down, sit down, Morgan. Don't let Martha get under your skin. She behaves very badly, it's quite a joke around the department.

MARTHA Don't clench your teeth so audibly, George. Come, come Morgy dear, you musn't run away now. Sit down like George told you to and we'll have a martini. *(She pulls a tiny jar of nuts from her bag and sets it on the table; then a huge bottle of gin which she takes into the kitchen. Sounds of shaking and crashing around from that quarter.)*

MONTELLE   Have another cigarette?

PIKE   Thanks. *(There is an uncomfortable silence; Pike looks gloomily out at the falling rain)* Professor Montelle, I'd like to ask your opinion on something.

MONTELLE   Certainly.

PIKE   Do you remember when I mentioned to you the other day my idea about abstracting some of the education material we get at Abbotsford?

MONTELLE   Yes, I remember.

PIKE   Well, I brought it up to Mr. Hathaway today and he was very discouraging about it.

MONTELLE   Oh?

PIKE   He felt it wouldn't be used, that it would be a waste of my time. But I felt that you had rather liked the idea.

MONTELLE   Well . . . didn't sound like a bad idea when you first mentioned it.

PIKE   But is it true that the faculty doesn't use these bibliographic tools? Would you use an abstract like this?

MONTELLE   Hmm . . . I'll have to admit, I use abstracts hardly at all myself.

PIKE   What do you use then?

MONTELLE   It depends, really, on what kind of information I'm looking for. Certainly, to keep up to date, I have to read the main Education journals, book reviews, that sort of thing. I do use *Education Index* occasionally for research, but I find that a lot of interesting tips on material come from my colleagues.

PIKE   Mr. Hathaway did say you people relied a lot on a "verbal exchange."

MONTELLE   Yes, we do . . . goes on all the time. It keeps us current on new ideas, new techniques. And this isn't just in the field of Education, you know. It's true generally that most published material *follows* an advance in a field.[1]

---

[1] "Advanced researchers seldom appear to draw their insights or inspiration from the literature." Paul Wasserman, *The Librarian and the Machine.* Detroit. Gale Research Co., 1965. p. 52.

PIKE   I suppose that's true. But still, there is an awful lot of published material you must have to keep abreast of. Surely you don't depend on this personal contact entirely?

MONTELLE   Of course not.

PIKE   Well, what do you depend on then?

MONTELLE   There is no one thing, of course; there are many ways of doing this: original research articles, newsletters of work being done, long informative reviews, reports of meetings, conferences themselves. Then we do make some use of indexes and abstracts for locating older material, but one thing that's particularly helpful is the trend to bibliographic essays these days. For instance, there was a whole issue of the *Wilson Library Bulletin* recently devoted to these. I happened to see it because there was one on Education.[2]

MARTHA   *(Coming out with the drinks)* Well! What is this scintillating conversation all about? *(She throws herself into a chair and pitches her shoes at the trash basket)*

PIKE   *(Laughs nervously and raises his glass)* Cheers.

MONTELLE   We're discussing methods of research, my dear. Morgan, here, has some ideas for aiding our Education department.

MARTHA   All that department needs is a kick in the ass.

MONTELLE   Martha!

PIKE   Perhaps I'd really better—

MARTHA   Siddown sweetie! Didn't the professor tell you not to let me under your skin? *(She laughs)* That's not *quite* where I'd like to be, but it's close.

MONTELLE   Cigarette?

PIKE   Thanks! *(He takes it gratefully and subsides on the sofa)*

MONTELLE   Martha, couldn't you fix some hors d'oeuvres or something?

MARTHA   Certainly, darling. *(Sweetly)* I'll just be a moment. *(She skips into the kitchen, slamming the door.)*

MONTELLE   Martha can be quite witty, you know. She's always in demand for the faculty show.

PIKE   Really? *(He can't think of anything else to say so repeats)* Really?

MONTELLE   *(Nervously pours another round)* Well—to go back to your question on research, there's a great deal of information being put out

---

[2] Fred Hechinger, "Books in the Field," *Wilson Library Bulletin*, XLI (November, 1966) pp. 311-317.

by the Government all the time, some of which is excellent and very helpful.

PIKE   Yes, I know. We have a lot of the bibliographic lists and indexes the Office of Education puts out and now there's this new development, Education Research Information Center, that's starting—to distribute reports from these special research centers.

MONTELLE   Ah yes, ERIC. I've been hearing about that. Do you have any of these reports?

PIKE   We have a few; frankly I haven't requested many because of reservations I've had about the program. And I don't like this microfiche.

MONTELLE   I've heard that some excellent work is being done—perhaps we can all learn how to handle the microfiche.

PIKE   But most of this material is abstracted and you've just been telling me that you don't want abstracts.

MONTELLE   But this is a very different kind of thing from your proposal. Each one of these centers has special and experienced people in the field, and they bring the process of selection to the material *before* it gets to the library.

PIKE   After all, I have a masters in ed.

MONTELLE   *(Sweeping on and disregarding Pike's gloom)* This whole new development of these different specialized centers is a very hopeful thing in my opinion. The government is backing many of them and they can afford the expensive research and equipment. Think of the possibilities for the smaller libraries!

PIKE   *(Sadly)* You encouraged me, I thought, Sir, when I first suggested my idea.

MONTELLE   Perhaps I did a bit . . . but I really hadn't had time to think about it, you know. I do feel that Hathaway probably is right.

MARTHA   *(Entering with a large cheese and some chips on a tray)* You look conspiratorial; I hope you're planning something "disloyal, disrespectful and subversive." *(She refills the glasses)*

PIKE   *(Who is getting excited)* I suppose you agree then about the computer, too? We should just sit around and "wait for the computer" and all our problems will disappear?

MARTHA   Sit down, sweetie, no point getting all worked up over a computer. Ugh! Why don't you bum another cigarette—it's good for George to feel needed.

MONTELLE   Why don't you just shut up, Martha! Morgan and I are having a very fruitful discussion. *(Pours another drink for Pike who looks bewildered; then, with a shrug, sits down)*

MARTHA   Well, I can't fix any more hors d'oeuvres, George, unless you can choke down that whole cheese. I'm afraid you can't get rid of me. *(She puts on a record and hums in her most irritating manner)*

MONTELLE   *(Returning doggedly to the topic)* I don't agree with Hathaway at all if that's his opinion. The possibilities of the computer are enormous—

MARTHA   Makes the mind boggle, doesn't it dear.

MONTELLE   But we're a long way from that world at Abbotsford. Even the biggest libraries and these special centers we've been talking about are still experimenting. There are a lot of problems—

MARTHA   Here's to all the lovely computers, clicking away with all the vital information!

MONTELLE   *(Ignoring Martha)* Have you read Gerald Hawkins' book about Stonehenge?

PIKE   No, I haven't.

MONTELLE   Well, one of the things that's so interesting about the book is the fact that Hawkins realized the immense possibilities of the computer for doing comparisons and calculations that it would take astronomers months, even years to do. They primed the computer with all sorts of information on position of celestial bodies and the different points of view from Stonehenge—don't ask me to explain the astronomy because I can't—

MARTHA   How touchingly humble!

MONTELLE   But it was the speed of the computer that made it possible for them to see all these significant alignments so quickly.

PIKE   Of course, I realize that computers will have a great impact on research. Mr. Hathaway seems to feel that this computer-produced "Index Medicus" is the guide that points the way.

MONTELLE   That's this MEDLARS?

PIKE   Yes, actually, "Medical Literature Analysis and Retrieval System." The National Library of Medicine had a "long standing literature control system,"[3] and had been putting out "Index Medicus". They switched to a computer in the attempt to have a very comprehensive coverage,

---

[3] Wasserman, *op.cit.* p. 82.

better depth as well, and of course, much greater speed. So far, it seems to have been very successful.[4]

MONTELLE   I imagine the centralization at one library has eliminated all sorts of duplication as well.

PIKE   Yes, and people see it at the center of a national system.[5] Like Mr. Hathaway, they see it as a model for other systems, but I'm not so enthusiastic myself.

MONTELLE   Why?

PIKE   Well, for one thing, the situation in which MEDLARS came about was rather special and might not be so easy to duplicate.

MONTELLE   It's true, of course—the index was a going concern already—

PIKE   And it lent itself pretty well to a changeover to machine because of the exact and scientific nature of the index already.

MONTELLE   There's a long road ahead for most of the social sciences before anything like this could develop, but I think it's a very good push in the right direction.

PIKE   But I feel that Mr. Hathaway, and others like him, haven't considered the other side of computers—sure we can be a lot more comprehensive and do it more quickly; but do we *want* to cover so much? I mean, is all this information necessary?

MARTHA   (*Rising dizzily and waving her glass*)

"All our knowledge brings us nearer to our ignorance,
All our ignorance brings us nearer to death,

* * * * * *

Where is the wisdom we have lost in knowledge?
Where is the knowledge we have lost in information?"[6]

(*She collapses on the sofa and begins to snore gently*)

MONTELLE   Martha puts it rather dramatically doesn't she? But you've

---

[4] "It joins the intellectual talents of professional literature analysts to the tremendous . . . capabilities of an electronic computer." Charles Austin, "The MEDLARS Project of the National Library of Medicine," *Library Resources and Technical Services,* IX (Winter, 1965) p. 94.

[5] "The truly dramatic feature of the program is the view which it permits of the way in which a national bibliographic system capable of performing high speed searching will be possible." Wasserman, op.cit. p. 84.

[6] T. S. Eliot, "Choruses from 'The Rock'" 1, *Collected Poems* (1909-1935) Harcourt, Brace & World, Inc., 1930. p. 179.

got a good point. Actually, it's not a new question. *(He picks up a magazine from the table)* There's an amusing article in here that brings up Jonathan Swift's approach to the problem in "Gulliver's Travels". Let me read you this.

"When Lemuel Gulliver went to the airborn, magnetic island of Laputa, you will remember, he came across a class of philosophers working in what seemed to be a sort of primeval Rand corporation. One of their study projects—no doubt financed by the 18th century equivalent of NASA—was a sort of information retrieval . . . which follwed a simple plan. All the possible words and phrases of the Laputa language were written on a sort of abacus-bead arrangement and the beads were strung on a wire frame, so constructed that they could move freely and randomly about. Laputan apprentices shook the frames; Laputan professors—or documentation experts—scanned the combination of words and phrases that resulted, and whenever they came across a line or a part of a line that made sense, they copied it down in a great book. It was their hope that in that way every bit of possible knowledge would be discovered and preserved—and put to use.

How it all worked out, Dean Swift does not say, but it seems very likely that what happened, after all was that they now had to begin finding a way of retrieving essentials out of the copious quantities of information they had already retrieved."[7]

(Both men drink reflectively, Martha snores)

PIKE   It's not just the problem of discriminating either—it's also the way computers and computer produced material has to be questioned.

MONTELLE   You're right. Questions have to be well defined—people have to know what they're looking for—and, of course, this isn't always the case. There's a good deal of random searching and accidental discovery that goes on. But the computer can save us so much time in many ways that it should give us more time for this other kind of searching—and perhaps for thinking!

PIKE   But what good is all this new world of computers and special centers going to do us here at Abbotsford?

---

[7] Fred Pohl, "Information Science-Fiction or Fact?," *American Documentation,* XVI (April, 1965) p. 102.

MONTELLE   Probably, more than you think; a lot more. As this kind of idea grows and physical access to material in central libraries gets quicker, we'll be able to send for a lot of good papers, reports, bibliographies—all sorts of material that we wouldn't ordinarily know about, much less be able to get now. And remember that there will have been human discrimination brought to bear on this; it's not just something fed raw into the computer.

PIKE   I guess we'll all have to get used to all these different copying techniques; microfilm, microfiche and so forth.

MONTELLE   That's right—and you could do the department a real service, Morgan, by finding out more about what may be available right now, from ERIC for instance, and sending for as much of it as you think our library can use.

PIKE   You really think this stuff would be used?

MONTELLE   If people knew about it and it was an accessible as the books and journals; of course they would.

PIKE   Well, perhaps I could try to keep some sort of listing of all types, that comes in each month—though I'd still continue to scan the most important items.

MONTELLE   I think that's a very good idea—really much more useful than the abstract. *(Martha wakes up and stares at them)*

PIKE   You've given me some good ideas. I do appreciate—

MARTHA   I can't stand this dull conversation a minute longer! Come and dance with me, Morgy.

PIKE   I should be going, really.

MARTHA   Well! Are you going to be rude? Come on, sweetie-pie, come to your Aunt Martha.

MONTELLE   Do leave him alone! *(Pike starts for the door)*

MARTHA   Morgy! You're serious? You're really going to leave me here with this bastard?

PIKE   *(Grabbing his coat and running out the door)* Thank you so much —so kind of you to invite me—goodnight—goodnight.

MARTHA   What a skunk!

MONTELLE   *(Wearily)* You're impossible, Martha—I've told you and told you—

MARTHA   And you're a double skunk! *(She picks up the cheese and hurls it at him. He ducks and it lands in the basket)* Ah! Perfect retrieval!

CURTAIN

Additional Bibliography

Bergen, Daniel, "Bibliographic Organization in the Social Sciences," *Wilson Library Bulletin*, XL (April, 1966) pp. 751-758.

Black, Donald, "Automatic Classification and Indexing for Libraries." *Library Resources and Technical Services*, IX (Winter, 1965) pp. 35-52.

Hawkins, Gerald, (in collaboration with John B. White), *Stonehenge Decoded*. New York. Dell Publishing Co., Inc. 1965.

Library Journal, XCI (September 1, 1966) p. 3891. (About ERIC).

Library Journal, XCI (October 15, 1966) p. 5144. (About ERIC).

Menzel, Herbert, "The Information needs of Current Scientific Research," *Library Quarterly*, XXXIV (January, 1964) p. 14.

Montgomery, Christine and Swanson, Don, "Machine-like Indexing by People," *American Documentation*, XIII (October, 1962), pp. 359-66).

Schiller, Hillel, 'What is MEDLARS," *Library Journal*, LXXXVIII (March 1, '63) pp. 949-953.

Taube, Mortimer, "Information Technology, Problems and Promises," *Library Journal*, XCI (March 1, 1966) pp. 1155-1158.

Uytterschaut, L., "Literature Searching Methods in Social Science Research," *American Behavioral Scientist*, IX (May, 1966).

Voigt, "The Researcher and his Source of Information," *Libri*, IV (1950) p. 190.